WHO WILL

DRIVE THE BUS?

Guidance for Developing Leaders
in the Family Enterprise

Gerard J. Donnellan PhD

First Edition January 2011

ISBN: 1456379909
ISBN-13: 9781456379902

Printed in the United States of America

Praise for *Who Will Drive the Bus?*

Drawing on his experience in working with business-owning families, Gerry has written a highly readable and practical book for family business leaders and professionals who advise family businesses. His use of case vignettes is a particularly effective way to help the reader understand common issues families face as they plan for succession in the family business. I recommend Gerry's book for anyone who is looking for effective ways to manage the family dynamics associated with creating a family enterprise designed to be sustainable over multiple generations of family ownership.

Stephen P. Miller, Vice Chair of the Executive Committee and Executive Vice President, The Biltmore Company, Asheville, North Carolina. Lecturer, Family Enterprise Institute, Center for Entrepreneurial Studies Kenan-Flagler Business School, University of North Carolina at Chapel Hill.

Gerry Donnellan has accomplished just what he sets out to do, to "help families navigate the sometimes murky waters of family businesses." But he does much more than that in this thoroughly readable book. He offers the reader practical suggestions, tools, and resources to navigate those waters and he does this with humor and wisdom. Who Will Drive the Bus? should be in every family business's library!

Jane Hilburt Davis, President, *Key Resources*, Cambridge, MA; Former President, *Family Firm Institute*.

Dr. Donnellan's book brings to life the steps that family business owners can take to develop the leadership critical for the business to prosper over generations. It highlights not only the importance of wise leadership, but offers practical steps that can be taken to develop that leadership. This is a book that every family business leader should own and read.

Henry Krasnow, Partner, *Krasnow Saunders Cornblath, LLP*. Chicago, IL.

With true-to-life war stories from the trenches, Gerry Donnellan provides meaningful fodder for dialogue and exercise around leadership development. His in-depth experience is heartened by passion for business family members to more than simply endure Thanksgiving dinner. His understanding of lasting change and the underlying issues endemic to family business present us with a prescription for this life-long process. Much more for the activist than for the passive observer, Gerry delivers a clear and concise hands-on guide that inspires a commitment to action. This is a "must read" for family business stakeholders.

Paul Karofsky, Founder and CEO, *Transition Consulting Group, Ltd.* **Palm Beach Gardens, FL. Executive Director Emeritus, Northeastern University Center for Family Business.**

Who Will Drive the Bus? *introduces the reader to the stories of seven business families. Family stories are one of the most effective ways to share what works well and what might work better as families develop the next generation to assume leadership positions. Using their stories as a point of departure, Dr. Donnellan shares valuable tools for readers to consider in their own situations. Also included are a helpful list of recommended resources, tips for running family meetings and a list of family business centers in the United States and Canada. This book gives families plenty of food for thought and many helpful tools for addressing the challenges and opportunities families face as they prepare the next generation for leadership roles in the future.*

Bonnie Brown Hartley, President, *Transition Dynamics Inc.* **Venice, FL.**

⌘ ⌘ ⌘

*Families are like fudge...
mostly sweet, with a few
nuts thrown in.*

~ A Yet-To-Be-Named Wise Person

Contents

Acknowledgements

I want to thank my colleagues and friends who have supported this project and provided guidance and thoughtful criticism at various points.

Paul Karofsky, Jane Hilburt Davis, Henry Krasnow, Lew Stern, Bob Burbidge, Douglas Chamberlain, Patricia Annino, Br. Rene Roy, John Davis, Lloyd Linford, Dave Hammerman, Sylvia Hammerman, Michael Madera, Victoria Nessen Kohlasch, Jennifer Ash, Harry Levinson, Detlev Suderow, Andrew Salmon, Bonnie Brown Hartley, Steve Miller, Jim O'Neil and Eileen Kelly.

My colleagues at the *Family Firm Institute*, members of my study group, and everyone at Psychosocial Dynamics of Family Business.

I want to thank Judy Green at the *Family Firm Institute* for providing me with the most complete list of family business centers in the United States and Canada. FFI has been a professional home for me for many years and for this, I am grateful.

Most especially, I want to thank my family: Hillary, Max, Corey, and little baby Annabelle, who, although she cannot yet read, offered her own kind of support in lots of smiles, giggles, and great wonderment at life. Most of all, I want to thank Suzanne, my wife and my partner in crime since man first walked on the moon. A terrific writer, grammarian, and honest critic, she knows what is important in life: family, friends, dogs, babies, and hot chocolate *mit schlag*.

⌘ ⌘ ⌘

Introduction

Family businesses are the heart, soul, and economic engine of much of the world. Even in the worst of times, they seem to find a way to survive—sometimes at great cost to family health and harmony. With guts, love, and a little luck, they will continue to be the source of tremendous innovation and creativity in the United States and global economies. They seem to find a way through the inevitable transitions.

If you are part of a family business, you are always dealing with transition: getting through one, getting over one, preparing for one, denying one is going to happen, or wishing you did not have to deal with one. More than any other type of business, a business that involves family members has at least three competing and interacting dynamics at work all the time: the family, the business, and the governance structure. Achieving stability that leads to growth in the business and harmony in the family is no mean feat. Many family businesses never quite achieve that harmony.

This book is meant for all those family businesses currently dealing with or about to deal with major transitions in the leadership of their firms. Our spotlight is on the leadership dimension of a succession plan. Any transition planning process involves many components and interlocking parts. These include a business strategic plan, the founder's personal financial plan, the family's mission statement, and the owner's estate plan. The development of the next generation of leaders should be a part of the strategic plan for the business.

This book is also written for families who want to stay in business together. These families and their businesses face unique and sometimes daunting challenges as they move forward from one generation to the next. Most (around 70 percent) do not make it past the first generation. The statistics speak for themselves:

- Eighty percent of the world's businesses are family owned.
- In just the past few years, Americans have started more than three million family businesses.

- Family-run businesses account for half of the nation's gross domestic product.

- Nearly 35 percent of Fortune 500 companies are family-controlled businesses, including Ford, Wal-Mart, and Toyota.

- Approximately 60 percent of all public companies in the United States are family controlled.

- Family-owned businesses account for 60 percent of total U.S. employment, 78 percent of all new jobs, and 65 percent of all wages paid.

- Many family businesses were started after WWII.

- There has been a significant increase in new family businesses since September 11, 2001.

- More than 30 percent of all family-owned businesses survive through the second generation. Twelve percent will still be viable into the third generation, with 3 percent of all family businesses operating at the fourth-generation level and beyond.

- Thirty-four percent of family firms expect the next CEO to be a woman; fifty-two percent of participants hire at least one female family member full time, while 10 percent employ two female family members of the same status.

- **Of CEOs due to retire within five years aged sixty-one or older, 55 percent have not yet chosen their replacement.**[1]

Yes, **55 percent have not yet chosen their replacement.** No wonder one of the biggest concerns for most families that work together is the issue of succession in the business. Many first-generation entrepreneurs act as if they will live forever and thus do not heed the advice from their own family and their own trusted advisers that they need to attend to the succession issue for the good of the business. Often, the pleas of those who care for them and for the business fall on deaf ears. This denial, narrow-

---

1 Reference materials include: Mass Mutual Family Business Survey 2007; Dr. Joseph H. Astrachan, Director of the Cox Family Enterprise Center; The University of Southern Maine's Institute for Family-Owned Business.

mindedness, and arrogance lead many successful business owners down the paths of their own destruction and the destruction of the business. It is all a shame and a terrible waste.

This book is written to help these families in each generation to navigate the murky and sometimes treacherous waters surrounding them. It is not easy to develop the next generation to take over or at least play a significant leadership role in the family business. As we often see, whether a small business or a giant one, the issues remain pretty much the same: old, unresolved issues from long ago rear their heads and interfere with good decision making and developing clearheaded strategies for moving the business forward.

My hope is that you will find this book useful immediately in your business and in your family. It is meant to create discussions and communications for you. I have tried not to be too preachy, although there is an element of "being the expert" that does creep in. I want you to use this book as a starting point or a drafting table from which you can develop your own blueprints that will work in your own particular circumstance of business and family.

Use this book as a transition guide as you consider the leadership needs for your firm. There are no facile prescriptions or bromides here. Rather, use this book to think about and consider what might work for you. My hope is that you will find some useful ideas for you and your business.

The chapters and the headings within them are arranged in line with the concerns that I hear from the families with whom I work. In each chapter you are introduced to a family and their business. These cases are fictitious, but they do represent what I have heard and keep hearing from these families. Their challenges are similar to many other families, but nonetheless very real and sometimes overwhelming to the family and the business. These families and their stories help introduce the themes developed in the rest of each chapter. The drama of their lives, sometimes so poignant and troubling, is real to them. I hope that you will be able to relate to them and their challenges, as you may see something of yourself in them.

This book is not encyclopedic in scope. This is a book written for you and your family. It is also meant to help you keep an eye on the sometimes swollen heads of those around you (including maybe your own!) and help everyone wear a normal-sized hat, at least in the business.

Have fun!

Gerry Donnellan

The Families

This book is about families and the decisions they make about the futures of their businesses. The fictitious families who are the focus of each chapter have particular challenges they must deal with as a family.

These are the families you will meet.

1. Erickson Family

When Carl dropped dead, everything stopped.

2. Cleary Family

Mary is diagnosed with Alzheimer's disease.

3. Morelli Family

A business started by new immigrants, the *Bambino Carriage Company* becomes a great success.

4. Sparks Family

The members of the Sparks family are unified in their commitment to building *Sparks Family Enterprises*, doing good, and giving back to the community.

5. Barbosa Family

The family restaurant blossoms and thrives.

6. Bluestone Family

A multigenerational family is infused with selfishness, arrogance, and small-mindedness.

7. Gladney Family

A family rooted in hard work, tradition, and strong will, the Gladneys build a business that spans four generations.

⌘ ⌘ ⌘

One

Wrestling for Dollars

The Ericksons

Nobody expected Carl Erickson to drop dead on the plant floor. The CEO of *Erickson Sealants* was sixty-seven years old and in good health. A massive heart attack was the last thing on anyone's mind. Candy, his wife, has had trouble coping since then, with the devastating loss of her complicated and gifted entrepreneur of a husband and also with the children in their blended family.

Carl's children from his first marriage, Carl Jr. (forty), and Robert (thirty-eight), are in the business. Carl Jr. earned his engineering degree at Carnegie Mellon and serves as the COO. Robert earned a PhD in chemistry from Cornell and heads up research and development. Candy (fifty-five) is Carl's second wife. She had been Carl's secretary; they married soon after he divorced his first wife. Her fraternal twin children, Sloane (thirty-two) and Sandy (thirty-two), both work in the business, as does Sloane's life partner, Sidney (thirty-one). The twins, both Harvard MBAs, run sales and marketing. Sloane covers the eastern United States and Europe, and Sandy covers the western United States and Asia. Sidney serves as CIO.

Carl Jr. and Robert both resent Candy because of the divorce. They refer to her as "the home wrecker." There is a long history of rivalry and bad feeling among the siblings. Carl Sr. encouraged what he called "healthy competition" among the siblings, even in the workplace. A brilliant and often irascible man, he held strong opinions about everything and demanded only the best from all around him.

After Carl's death, things came to a head when Carl Jr. and Sloane, after yelling and screaming at each other, wrestled on the plant floor in front of employees. Several employees had to pull them apart. It was a messy scene. The conflicts and resentments between the children and the stepchildren have only worsened since then. There has been spill over into the offices and in the plant since "the big fight," as employees refer to it. Rumors have been flying that the plant would close, that the company was on the auction block, or that there was court fight with family members suing each other.

The situation

After earning his PhD at MIT, Carl Sr. developed the formulas for chemical adhesives that are now used in everything from flypaper to construction supplies, high tech military equipment, and consumer goods. The company started out in his garage and has evolved into a successful company ($150 million in sales in FY 2010). However, due to the economic downturn, sales have steadily declined.

This certainly was not the scenario Carl envisioned for his baby, *Erickson Sealants.*

Candy holds the controlling interest in the company, with other shares evenly divided among Carl's biological children and the stepchildren. She asked the nonfamily CFO to run the company until they could figure out what to do.

The major issue was that there was no succession plan nor had there been any open discussion about transitions in the company. Any proposed leadership development plan or activities always were put on the back burner, as Carl only focused on immediate concerns. With all the squabbling and rumors, the business was suffering because no one was sure what direction to take.

Carl's "little baby," was in big trouble.

So what happened?

The "little baby" grew up. The company did well under Carl's leadership and control. But, as he grew older and the business was no longer a *little* baby, he never addressed the issue of passing it on to the next generation. "I'll outlive all of you!" he said. It did not quite work out that way.

Underlying all of the business challenges was the many past problems and unspoken family issues, such as Carl's boys harboring resentment toward Candy. The history of rivalry among the siblings vying with each other for their father's attention and approval only fueled the fires.

This was a classic case of "no succession planning."

How could things have been different and what do they do now?

There are several issues to consider:

- **Succession planning is not a one-time deal.** It is a process that takes time, patience, and lots of consideration. It involves all the parties working in a collaborative way to focus on the needs of the enterprise, as opposed to their own self-interest. This is no mean feat.

- **The kids cannot make it happen.** It must be driven and championed by the senior leaders.

- **Developing leaders is only one component of the succession planning process.**

- **Leaders must be identified, developed, nurtured, and "brought along."** Best practices suggest that for the next generation to be truly in a position to lead, they must know the business inside and out, and have had a range of experience both inside the family business and outside— maybe even in other industries.

- **The odds of success should be much greater than "*crossing your fingers and hoping for the best.*"** The heart of the process is the plan and the commitment to developing the next generation leaders in a way that will ensure their success, optimize their talents, and allow them to find and grow into the role that best suits them. As a family business executive once said to me, "Well, it's his turn to be CEO. We all take turns—that's how we do it." Needless to say, this was not the best, nor the most prudent, way to choose the top leadership of the company. Blood and the right genes does not make up for lack of talent or lack of fit for the position.

This brings us to the issue of what leadership development is and how it fits into the overall transition planning process.

What is a leader?

There is a billion-dollar industry in the United States devoted to providing programs, training, books, magazines, and executive coaching aimed at developing business leaders. Each offering claims to be the right path to effective leadership. Is it any wonder that

> **Leader**
> One who wields commanding influence.[2]

many businesses fail to move on developing their leaders? Faced with so many choices and little guidance about what is appropriate and useful for their particular set of circumstances, most businesses don't know what to do.

Carl believed that there was no one who could do what he did, and therefore, he would just keep doing it. Indeed, he was the one with the most influence, yet he failed to lead in a most crucial and fundamental way. If he really wanted to ensure his legacy, he would have done everything in his power to transition the business to the next generation. Perhaps he died too soon and failed to fulfill his dream.

A Leadership Development Model

The model below illustrates the range of activities for developing family business leaders. This serves as framework that we will use throughout the book. There are three major areas or approaches for developing family business leaders: **people, experiences, and programs**. Ideally, each is integrated with the other. A developing leader, for example, will have experience in another company before joining the family business; will undertake more formal education or coursework related to the business, perhaps in marketing or finance; and finally, will have a range of helpful relationships with mentors in and outside the company to advisers such as executive coaches and family members.

---

2 Webster Unabridged International Dictionary

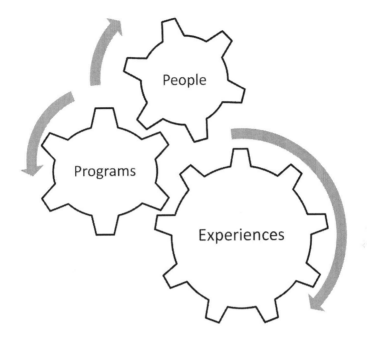

Figure 1-1: The Family Business Leadership Model

- **People**
  - Family

    There are many resources within the family who can be helpful to developing leaders. Starting with Mom and Dad, each one can contribute something to shaping the children as leaders. If mom works in the business, she can be a tutor/mentor about what she does, what her role has been in the business, what skills she has, and how she has developed in her career.

    The same is true for Dad. If he is the head of the company, he can be of tremendous value to the kids by being generous with his time and knowledge. This includes not only discussing his role with each child but also allowing each child to spend time with him as he performs that role. Parents' efforts to prepare their progeny for possible careers in the business must begin before the children graduate college or when they are ready to join the business. It starts when they are children by introducing them to the business. It also starts by having conversations with them about work, about the business as a family business, and about the history of the business.

Preparing the next generation for leadership roles does not begin when they are in their forties! Other members of the family can serve as role models and resources to the next generation. Aunts, uncles, and cousins,whether they are connected to the business or not can have something to teach the children about work, the family, and the values of the family.

o Mentors

If the business is large enough, there should be leaders in the business who can take Johnny or Sally under their wing to teach them about the business and their role in it. This kind of direct mentoring relationship can have enormous impact, as the older person teaches something about his or her role, the business, and his or her experience.

Mentors serve as models for their *mentees* (as they are called). As models, they literally can show the younger person the ropes. More than anything, however, a good mentor shows the path he or she has taken and is willing to discuss what it takes to be successful and how to grow in the business.

o Advisers

There are many advisory relationships that can be of great use to developing leaders. Some of these are:

- ▪ Executive Coaching: As we will discuss in the detail in chapter 4 with the Sparks family, the role of the executive coach can add real value in developing the next geneeration of leaders.

- ▪ Presentation Coaching: As a leader moves up in the organization, there are more opportunities to present to audiences inside and outside the business. At some point, many business leaders need some "sprucing up" of their presentation skills. For example, many leaders are unaware of how they may come across to an audience and may believe that their presentations are "just fine" when, in fact, they may not engage the audience very well, may mumble when they speak, or are boring in some way. A presentation coach can help with all of these issues.

- **Experiences**

  o <u>Outside the business:</u> Many families now have agreements that stipulate that any member of the next generation who wishes to enter the business must have x number of years of experience outside the business before they will be considered for employment in the business. These employment agreements serve two functions: they make it clear what the expectations are for entering the business, and they place great value on other experience, training, and education before that person can enter the business. As business has become more complex, more family businesses are doing this.

  o <u>In the business</u>: Many development plans for potential leaders require individuals to spend time in each area of the business; this allows them to learn about the entire business in a real way. In more savvy family businesses, there is an appreciation for the value of experience in the business, from the top to the bottom. A recent TV show featured a CEO working at a lower-level job within his company, such as emptying trash barrels or serving hamburgers in the restaurant. Each CEO came away with the same reaction: "I never knew how tough these jobs were. I was so disconnected from my own people that I had no idea things were so tough."

  o <u>Life:</u> Younger family members working in the business may benefit from rubbing shoulders with more senior leaders. The very fact of working with Uncle Bob on the shop floor gives the younger person a perspective that he or she would never get if they spent all their time up in the office.

Some young people do need to spend some time "out in the world" discovering something about themselves, their interests, and abilities. This is not to be ignored. For example, a young member of a family business had spent some time living and working in Honduras, both in college and for a year after. This experience gave her a perspective on living that could not be gained in any other way than by living it. When a younger person brings that into the family business, the family and the business are much richer for it.

- **Programs**
  - <u>General business programs</u>: Many university-based business programs offer an array of instruction in general business, leadership, management, and other areas. These might be explored as part of developing an overall plan for the emerging family business leaders.

  - <u>Family business focused programs:</u> There are several family business centers in the United States, Mexico, and Canada that are housed in a local university. In Boston, the *Northeastern University Center for Family Business,* for example, offers many outstanding programs for members of family businesses. Such centers offer programs for all the members of the family business, from the older generation to Generation 3 (G3) and beyond.

  - <u>Academic courses:</u> Education is crucial to success in the family business these days. Most children do not enter the business as entrepreneurs. They generally enter a more mature business that makes different demands on them. Continuing education of some sort is important because it keeps you aware of the latest ideas/trends in business, and it also expands your knowledge base. A young family member entering the family business with a BA in marketing, for example, may need to spend some time taking courses in finance or operations, or perhaps pursue an MBA.

o <u>Leadership development programs</u>: Leadership development opportunities are everywhere. Some are great and some are not so great. In choosing such programs, whether university-based or commercially offered, it is important to get references and talk with people who have taken them.

Leading is teaching

Some people learn from experience and others do not. The ones who find new, creative ways to apply what they have learned, and are willing and eager to share what they have learned are leaders. To lead is to teach.

In *True North*, Bill George focuses on authentic leaders—who they are, where they come from, and what drives them. One such leader is Dan Vasella, CEO of Novartis Pharmaceuticals. As a global multibillion-dollar company, Novartis is in a position to affect and help millions of people around the world. They develop medicines used in the fight against cancer, as well as other drugs. Dan Vasella leads a huge organization, yet his focus is clear and laser sharp. He knows what drives him and what is important to him. He said, "As CEO, I have the leverage to impact the lives of many more people. I can do what I believe is right, based on my moral compass. At the end of the day, the only thing that matters is what we do or [fail] to do for other people." (*True North*, p.49)

He is a person with a passionate, singular focus to improve the lives of as many people as he can by developing drugs that will help them. What is the source of his passion?

It derives from his childhood experiences in Switzerland. He suffered many illnesses as a young child and was away from his home for long periods. His sister died and shortly thereafter his father passed away. When he found his focus in medical school, the contours of his life plan began to emerge. Based on his own experience of loss and illness as a child, he was determined to do all he could to improve the lives of others. His quest eventually led him to the corner office of Novartis. He is driven by deeply held beliefs and what he refers to as his "moral compass." He has created a culture and "teaches by being" what is important to him and the company. Success is measured in lives saved.

As we consider the families in this book, we will meet some who have that passion, drive, and determination, and some who do not. In a family business, that passion and focus reside primarily in the founding entrepreneur whose hard work grew the business from nothing. The seed for this kind of leader is in the blood of the heirs who follow that inspirational leader. As we see all too often, however, many times those seeds fail to germinate.

I believe this type of leader—the inspired, passionate teacher— represents the new leadership that we see more and more in the business world. Some call them *the quiet leaders* who lead from behind or the *collaborative leader* or the *whispering influencer*. Whatever the term, these individuals have that *something* that makes people want to work with them and to excel at what they do. These leaders inspire trust and loyalty in those around them. They are authentic. They are the real deal.

Can this authenticity be learned or instilled in someone? Can you take a class in it? How does it happen? For some people it is *who they are*. They have lived their life like this. Others are individuals whose passion and direction flows from deep, life-changing experiences. They are driven, focused, and determined because of that experience. Whatever the internal driving force, they lead in an authentic way, in alignment with who they are and what they believe; they are focused on what they want to accomplish. The business and its success are important, but these leaders are far more concerned that the organization's goals be attained.

What we are seeing these days in the United States and beyond is a steady and not-so-subtle shift in the character of those who lead many of our companies and institutions. We now see that those with genuine passion and single-minded focus are successful and have successful enterprises. Being driven by ideals and living by them can actually be good business. Having a moral compass and living by it is not incompatible with doing well in the business world.

Family businesses should be promoting and developing their leaders in line with family values, culture, and the family legacy. Unfortunately, those that seem to get most into trouble are those family enterprises with weak, nonexistent, toxic, or destructive cultures and values. Of course, having a big pile of money on the table can make a bad situation worse.

Leading is influencing

Quiet leaders influence those around them. Another aspect of leadership, then, is the leader's ability to influence. We might define a leader, then, as, *"Someone who sets direction and influences others to follow that direction."*

In this vein, there are many theories about leadership, all of which emphasize one facet or another of our perspective here. Some of these theories are:

- Servant leader
- Democratic leader
- Principle-centered leader
- Group-man theory
- Great-man theory
- Traits theory
- Visionary leader
- Total leader
- Situational leader

The Leader
"Someone who sets direction and influences others to follow that direction."

Authenticity and collaboration

In the 2007 survey of business leaders conducted by the *Center for Creative Leadership* some interesting trends emerged. Respondents were asked to indicate the three skills they will need to be an effective leader in the future.

Only 50 percent of respondents believed senior leaders are currently able to be authentic in their role. Because trust and respect are vital in the workplace, developing these skills for the future will be essential to keeping the workforce engaged and committed over the long term.[3]

Collaboration (49 percent), change leadership (38 percent), building effective teams (33 percent), and influence without authority (33 percent) were at the top. The skills that ranked at the bottom—those deemed less important for the future—are ethical decision making (8 percent), credibility (9 percent), and straightforwardness and composure (10 percent). These results suggest that future leadership skills should emphasize building teams and relationships, collaboration, and change management.

More than 97 percent of senior leaders indicated that collaboration is essential to success. However, only 30 percent of respondents and 47 percent of senior leaders believed leaders in their organization are actually skilled in collaboration. These results suggest leaders must learn to work across boundaries to collaborate effectively in the coming years.

The survey noted, "Only 50 percent of respondents believed senior leaders are currently able to be authentic in their role. Because trust and respect are vital in the workplace, developing these skills for the future will be essential to keeping the workforce engaged and committed over the long term."

> Only 50 percent of respondents believed senior leaders are currently able to be authentic in their role. Because trust and respect are vital in the workplace, developing these skills for the future will be essential to keeping the workforce engaged and committed over the long term. *Center for Creative Leadership*, 2007 survey of business leaders.

These results support the idea that being authentic as a leader is not just a "nice thing to be" but is crucial for the health of the

---

3 Available at www.ccl.org

business. Many research studies in the last ten years offer proof that qualities such as loyalty, authenticity, genuineness, collaboration, and being a team player impact the business in a very positive way. When we talk about the Sparks family in a chapter 4, this point will be underscored.

Take a stand—be a champion

1. <u>Be the leader</u>—teach those around you. Since leading is all about teaching, be a teacher to those around you. Be eager to learn about yourself and what it is you need for your own development. Do not shy away from learning—it will make you stronger and better at your job. It will also set you apart from your competition.

2. <u>Commit yourself to your own development</u>: lead by example. Make the commitment to learn more and know why you are making that commitment. For example, Bob Burbidge, founder and CEO of *Genesis Consolidated Services*, decided to get an MBA because he recognized that it would enhance his decision-making, his understanding of his business and the market, and his competitive advantage. He says:

> When I went back to school, over thirty years had passed since I received my undergraduate degree. The world had changed so much in that time, and even though I had run a business for twenty-two years and achieved a fair measure of success, I knew it would be difficult to keep pace. While experience is undoubtedly the best teacher, many new investment-backed players were entering our space, bringing with them degrees from Harvard Business School, Wharton, and the like. They had the backing and the brains, and eventually they would get the experience.
>
> It was a wise decision for the company and a great experience for me. It certainly has

helped us weather the recession that began in 2008. Encouraging the development of the intellectual capital of our senior managers had long been the cornerstone of our business. I only wish I hadn't waited so long to commit to developing my own business and leadership skills.

3. <u>Who takes their own development seriously?</u> Not many. Why is that? Is it because it seems like a waste of time that could be spent on—what? It is the best investment you could make in the company that you and everyone else around you work in. Development should become part of the culture of the organization. All the "big boys" invest in their people because those people represent the future of the enterprise. Without them and without developing them, the business is doomed.

4. <u>What do champions do?</u>

- They practice harder than anyone else.
- They maintain absolute focus on the goal.
- They listen to their coach.

Champions accomplish things that many people fail to achieve. They excel in the face of heavy odds against them; they power on and "move to the next level" through determination, willpower, and the ability to see better than anyone what they need to do. In the real world, champions are incredibly persistent and sometimes pigheaded.

The champion stands for something and makes a commitment to it. If Carl had said, "We need to pay attention to developing the next generation of leaders," and had engaged others in the company to determine and implement a plan to accomplish that goal, that plan would have become an integral part of the

> **Champions**
> - Practice harder than anyone else.
> - Maintain absolute focus on the goal.
> - Listen to the coach.

business's culture and part of the strategic plan (something else many family businesses do not do.)

A word of caution

Even with tremendous passion and drive, a champion who is surrounded by people more focused on self-interest and their own political success may find his or her progress thwarted. Pettiness, self-centeredness, politics, *and money* make for a combustible mix, and it is usually the family business that blows up!

Develop realistic goals

Many leadership development efforts falter because at the outset there was no clear set of realistic goals. When the founder says, "I want Johnny to succeed me and that's that." This is not a plan but a directive. It merely is a statement to be followed by everyone around him. This leaves little room for any accommodation, discussion, or the inauguration of a leadership process. Worst of all, it demands nothing of Johnny. It is as if Johnny just has to bide his time, not make too many mistakes, and wait for the reins to pass to him. There are no expectations of him, nothing he needs to accomplish, and there is no vision or plan. This is not a good formula for business success.

Realistic goals are specific and attainable. Some might be:

- Develop expertise in production and marketing.
- Join the program in leadership development at the local university center for family business.
- Deepen one's knowledge of the entire professional services division.
- Spend time in the branch offices or the plant floor to see how they operate and get to know the people.
- Spend more effort to understand what the CFO does.
- Spend more time "walking around" and meeting the employees where they work. Don't just be seen at the holiday party.

Many of these goals appear simple and mundane but each contributes a share to growing one's identity, comfort, and competence as a leader. We will discuss these goals in detail in chapter 2.

Business impact

Ultimately, if a leadership development effort is to have any traction or credibility, it must impact the business in a real way. The big questions to be answered are:

- Will this effort and the money spent result in any competitive advantage in the marketplace? If yes, how much? If no, why not? What needs to change?

- Is this effort linked to the strategic initiatives of the enterprise? Real, sustainable leadership development efforts are closely linked to overall strategy. Carl Erickson, for example, could have spent some time with this senior team (all owners) to focus on strategy. That exercise would have achieved several goals:

  o It would have created a culture in which everyone is always linking what he or she does to the vision and strategy of the company.

  o If everything is considered in light of vision and strategy, there will be fewer bad moves. Leadership and developing the leadership team is just one more component of the overall strategy and will be less likely to get axed (as these things do) when belt-tightening is called for.

Priority #1

What is the number one priority for the business right now? Often this question gets lost in the shuffle of daily concerns and can fall to the bottom of the list. Here are some considerations to keep in mind if you are trying to figure out what the priorities of the business are right now:

- How is the business doing?

- What are the strengths, weaknesses, opportunities, and threats right now? Called a SWOT analysis, this kind of exercise can be very useful for taking a snapshot of the business and where it stands.

- Are you growing, stagnant, or losing in the marketplace? Why? Do you need to do anything to respond to this situation?

- Do you have the talent right now that you need to respond to this situation? Do you need to do anything about that?

- Where is the business in the business cycle? Is it growing like crazy, holding its own and doing okay, mature and holding on, or losing market share and on the decline?

- Do you expect to be selling the business, passing it on to the next generation, or just holding on until it implodes?

Preparation is key. Your answers to these questions will determine what your priorities are and what your next steps might be. Getting clear on priorities can go a long way toward answering some fundamental questions about the business, who should be leading it, and how that person or persons need to be prepared.

The road to Snoozetown

Several years ago I worked with a family business that had reached its fourth generation. In a market with thin profit margins, they had done well or at least well enough to show some profit each year. The shareholders were members of the extended family, who numbered well over fifty individuals, including all the cousins, spouses, and children. It was generally a family that got along well, liked to spend time with each other, and often got together for holidays, birthdays, and vacations. They had reached a crisis point, however.

The succession plan was simple: each sibling working in the business, who had spent considerable time in it and contributed to it, would take a turn at being CEO. In the current instance, however, there were serious, major concerns about the qualifications and competency of the person next in line. Although board members were very concerned about this predicament, they did feel that "right was right" and that he should have his turn at running the company. The advisers, including me, suggested that they consider alternatives, including appointing a nonfamily CEO to the position.

Eventually, genes won out, and the next in line was appointed CEO. The company managed to hang on, with significant help and guidance from the nonfamily leader who was the brains of the operation. They struggled, and there were a lot of bad feelings within the family that, despite the red flags, the person had become CEO. Family relations remain strained. Bitterness and resentment now haunt this once close family.

> **How do you know you are headed to Snoozetown?**
> - Genes win over merit.
> - Family members are more focused on their own interests than those of the business.
> - Strong feelings and conflicts go unresolved.
> - There is poor communication all around.

What was so bad? It was a poor decision. There were many things wrong here:

- Genes won out over merit and competence.

- The entire culture of the organization was set back because everyone in the company knew this was a poor choice.

- Once-committed family members/shareholders now stood off to the side and distanced themselves from the business; they became more concerned about the value of their shares and the number on the annual distribution. Protecting one's assets now prevailed

- The zip, zing, and fun of being a part of this family business slipped away. People had *jobs* and that was what they did. They were not really committed to the growth of the business. There was not a lot of creative problem solving or innovation going on.

They had boarded the bus to the land of the bored and sleepy: *Snoozetown.* This is the place where family businesses are headed after they have had a good run (maybe several generations), after the fun has left, and after nobody really cares that much about the business. They are mostly dozing off, waiting for the check. The shame of it all is that the business suffers, and the family suffers even more.

Choices

From the Ericksons to the inhabitants of *Snoozetown*, there are many choices on how best to grow the business and its leaders. The starting point is a commitment to taking a hard look at the future, thinking strategically about the business, putting a plan in place, and executing that plan.

⌘ ⌘ ⌘

Checklist

✓   If you want to preserve your "little baby", like Carl Erickson, take care of it.

✓   Get serious about developing emerging leaders before you cannot remember what serious means.

✓   Teach by example.

✓   Keep learning.

✓   Be realistic.

✓   Develop your priorities.

✓   Do not get on the bus to Snoozetown.

Two

Wednesday Matinees

Bill, Mary, and the Kids

Mary had always been the rock in the family. She had held the family together through all the bumps in the forty years that she and Bill were married. They had a good marriage, great kids, and now grandchildren to enjoy. In the months before the diagnosis, Mary seemed to be more forgetful and sometimes had difficulty recognizing friends whom she had known for many years. When the neurologist said that she had a form of early dementia, maybe Alzheimer's disease, both Mary and Bill could not believe it. In the ensuing months since then it became clear she had been was slowly going downhill for quite some time.

The children, Greg, Sandra, and Bill, Jr., each had a tough time seeing their mother losing ground. It was devastating to the family. The Sunday dinners at Mom and Dad's house became a bit more difficult, as each of the children took more responsibility for planning, cooking, and getting the meal on the table.

All of the kids, now in their late thirties, worked in the business, *Cleary's Floors*. They saw each other every day and spoke often about Mom and how she was doing. This was a close-knit family. They cared deeply for each other.

The business was doing well, and in recent years had topped its revenues by 8-10 percent annually. The business was growing and with Bill Jr. leading the way in the expansion of the rug cleaning and repair side of the business they were poised for significant growth. The $15 million business offered opportunities to the family and the employees for professional growth. Their core business, commercial hardwood floor installation and repair, had remained solid, in spite of the downturn in the economy.

Bill had always maintained good relationships with his children. They respected him both as a father and as a savvy businessman. The kids and their dad met every Wednesday for lunch and talked about the business, generated updates, and focused on the areas for improvement in each piece of the business. Recently, Bill had raised the issue about perhaps taking a less visible role in the company, paring back his time so he could spend more time with Mom and maybe play a little more golf. At sixty-two, he was in good health, watched his weight and exercised. Bill, Jr., Sandra, and Greg could not believe their ears as they had thought their dad would never step away from the business he loved. But things were different now. They would all have to pick up the slack and adjust. As Sandra noted, "We're going to have to figure this out together."

The "Wednesday matinees," as they called their lunch meetings, took on a more serious note as all four of them tried to have open discussions about their next steps for the business and for the family. No one was exactly sure what those steps might be, as there were many considerations, not the least of which was Mom's decline.

An old school buddy of Greg's had mentioned to him that the local university had a family business center that offered programs and meetings. Greg thought he might check it out, as the kids felt some pressure to get some input and direction for themselves and for the business. Fortunately, within a couple of weeks he attended a program on dealing with transitions in the family. When he attended as a guest, he found that the members talked quite freely about the challenges in their businesses and sought the input from other families. It seemed like a good place for his family to seek the input they needed.

Good for the organization

This was a good start for Greg and the family. Since they were all feeling the very real emotional strain of their mother's illness, they also realized that the implications for them and for the business were not to be ignored. In comparison to the Ericksons, they had a lot going for them, both in the business and the family. As a family, they were quite stable, engaged with each other, not divided by petty squabbles or old resentments, and most importantly, they were committed to each other. That commitment spilled over into the business and allowed their meetings to be focused on business issues, problem solving, and strategy development.

Greg had taken a first step. For many families that first step could be almost anything—reading a book, attending a local program, taking a course, talking with other family business owners, or just deciding to *do something*. Taking action is key, as Greg soon learned. He attended more meetings at the center and eventually invited both his brother, sister, and dad to join him; they felt that they had found a place where they could talk about things in an open forum with people who were dealing with similar issues. They were all quite relieved.

So why is doing something good for the organization?

- It gives the business leaders, the Cleary children and their dad in this case, a place to get things that are generally difficult to express out on the table.

- There is the mutual support and encouragement of other families.

- A system develops that provides members access to each other outside meetings in more social situations, which is often a good way to exchange ideas.

- The variety of programs and offerings can serve the varied needs of each family member. Sandra became good friends with another family business member who had kids about the same age as her children. Eventually, they talked more on the phone and would meet for lunch to talk about family, kids, and their businesses.

- The issues of transition, succession, and developing the leaders in the business can be addressed in such a way that often thorny issues surrounding these topics can be addressed in a more systematic and less anxiety-provoking way.

Mentor, teach, and develop your leaders

Gradually, over a couple of years, the picture of their options emerged for Bill and the children. During that time, he worked on his personal financial plan, undertook the estate planning process, and addressed Mary's long-term care needs, which were looming in the future.

The issue of passing the baton and who would be the next leader of the business soon emerged. Since they all had good, solid relationships with each other that could withstand the storms of disagreements and conflicts, they managed to get the issue out on the table. With help from a consultant they had met through another family business, they began a series of meetings to discuss the pros and cons of various alternatives. Ultimately, it became clear that Greg, who had spent almost his entire professional career within the business, was the most logical choice. He had been running operations since Dad had stepped away. He knew the business very well and seemed to have a knack for and comfort with "being in charge." Both Sandra and Bill Jr. supported this because they were pleased with the roles they were carving out for themselves in the business. Sandra ran the back office and was in charge of sales and marketing. Bill Jr. continued to grow the rug cleaning and repair side of the business.

With these steps, Greg, Sandra, and Bill Jr. each began learning more about the needs of the business, and what they needed as the next generation leaders. Bill Jr., for example, sought out the CEO of a company that was the same size as theirs and with whom he had become friendly. Over time this became more of a mentoring relationship, with Bill Jr. seeking out the advice and counsel of the more seasoned person.

What type of family business do you have?

The Clearys are a decent, hardworking family. They are good to each other, they care for Mom, and they work well with each other in the business and in the family. Although, no one is quite sure what percentage of family businesses are like the Clearys, we can hope that it is high. Given the fact that so many family businesses do not make it to the second generation, one has to wonder how much of that failure rate has to do with by the obstacles created by family dynamics.

So what kind of family business are you? Are you engaged with each other, good to each other, able to withstand conflict and disagreement, and open with each other? Or do old arguments, petty disagreements ("She ALWAYS got more than me!), and old fights drag you down?

The figure below is one tool I use to help families understand more about themselves and what kind of family they are. Although no family fits neatly into a particular box or category, many find themselves more or less in one area.

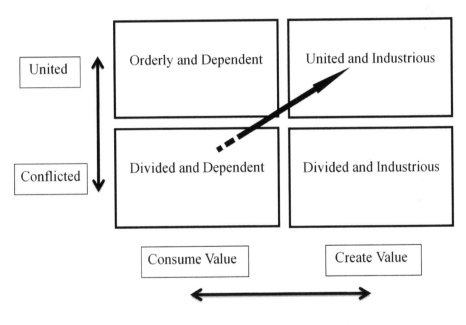

Many thanks to John Davis

Figure 2-1: Family Business Types

In this figure, there are two dimensions. On the lower, horizontal axis is the factor *create value or consume value in the business.* Some family members, for example, may not work in the business but may draw significant monies from the business. In other families, members work in the business and create value in the business not only by their work but also by their commitment to the enterprise.

On the left side is *united vs. conflicted.* This has to do with the emotional tenor or tone of the family. Are they, like the Clearys, committed to each other, the family, and the business, or do they tend to be more interested in their own personal gain and interests? In New England, for example, one very large family business was pulled apart and devastated by the rancor and bitterness of the warring brothers who spent years in court and millions of dollars trying to beat each other up. In the end, they mostly supported the tennis courts and club memberships of their respective lawyers. Neither brother achieved satisfaction in the courts over their perceived differences. They lost, the family lost, and the business certainly lost.

Take the pulse of the family.

It always helps to know what is on people's minds. Here is an example of a very brief survey I use with families. The survey helps get family members thinking about the present, the future, and the challenges they face right now. It is easy to set up online and responses

Dear Family,

There are several questions below. You may answer with as much detail as the space will allow. This survey is set up so that all the responses come directly to me. All responses are anonymous. Your name will not appear anywhere in connection with discussions of this survey. Honesty and "saying it like it is" is important. This should take fifteen minutes or so. It is best to just complete it in one sitting.

Thank you for your participation.

1. Please describe three great things about this family.

2. As a member of this family, what is most challenging to you right now?

3. What would you like to see improve for the family in the near future?

4. What is your "dream" for this family in the long term?

5. What do you think it would take for this dream to come true?

can be collected anonymously by a consultant or trusted person outside the family.

There are many different ways to look at the responses generated by this simple survey. Here is an example of the responses from one family. This was used in a family retreat to help the family focus on the present and stop complaining about the past.

⌘ ⌘ ⌘

Below are the results from the family survey. These are not necessarily a verbatim report of the responses, but in most cases are representative of the themes present in your answers to the questions posed. Please read them and think about them. We will use this as a platform for our meeting.

1. **Please describe three great things about this family.**

   - Our values and trying to live by them.
   - We continue to live, work, and celebrate together as a family.
   - Mom and Dad.
   - Our appreciation of our family history, goals, and shared values.
   - Good people—part of a close family. "Naturally giving" people.
   - The closeness of the kids; love between the families.
   - People engaged in life.
   - The "glue" of the grandkids.

2. **What is most challenging to you as a member of this family?**

   - Time pressure to connect.
   - Splitting into groups/polarities.
   - Tremendous tension and splitting into groups.
   - Being in a fishbowl in the world.
   - Personal feelings of pain, dishonesty, and distrust.

- Not getting the buy-sell (shareholder) agreements done.
- Can't even celebrate how well the business is doing.

3. **What would you like to see improve in the family in the near term?**

   - We are all going to have to come to the middle on this one. We should be responsible for the family and ourselves.
   - Genuine compromise and consensus on the shareholder agreement.
   - Achieving "real harmony" of the family over the business.

4. **What is your "dream" for this family in the long term?**

   - A balance between the business and the family. If we can do this, we will be closer and have fewer "issues" with which to deal.
   - For G2 and G3: respect and appreciation for each other as we grow older. For G4, to help them preserve and follow their interests and talents.
   - See the whole family get along together again.
   - Be role models for the next generation.

5. **What do you think it would take for this dream to come true?**

   - Honest communication. Tough choices. Time. A little faith. A little luck.
   - Establish shared values and expectations.
   - For each family member to accept, in a real way, his or her own responsibility for this mess.
   - I am not sure it is possible. Sounds like a pipe dream. Too much anger and distrust.

⌘ ⌘ ⌘

What have we learned about this family?

- They are highly conflicted at this moment in time.
- Some are discouraged and question whether change or resolution is possible.
- Many still hope that they will come togeher and resolve the current crisis.
- There are shareholder issues that are unresolved and have been so for some time.
- They mostly believe they have a good family, and are driven by and rooted in a strong family culture and values.
- They have not achieved the balance they want between the business and the family.
- They have been in business going into the fourth generation. The business is successful. They must be doing something right.

What don't we know?

- Are some family members consuming more value than they add?
- Who is in the business, and who is not?
- How are shares divided among family members? Is there a majority shareholder?
- How is the business affected by all this conflict (because it certainly has to be)?
- What will get their attention and make them change?

Returning to the framework of the family business types, let's consider the four possibilities based on the diagram:

- **Orderly and dependent**: This type of family gets along well and is not pulled apart by nastiness or bitterness. On the other hand, the family members don't add any value to the business and don't work particularly hard at anything. This is generally a family of nice people who are quite content to draw from the business and are not overly concerned about being engaged with the business, as long as the dividend checks arrive on time.

- **Divided and dependent**: These are not happy campers. They do not play well together. There are many side issues that they get caught up in. They will pay attention to the business and sometimes will interfere if it looks like they are not getting what they think deserve. Occasionally, these families get up in arms over the appointment of a new CEO or president, if that person actually attempts to rein them in. They are more concerned about their own self-interest than that of the business. They are dependent on the business and are content as long as that does not change.

- **Divided and industrious**: These people like to work and many times do work in the business, but they are not happy. There is always something wrong, and there is always someone to blame. They like to blame each other and do not seem to have much commitment to each other or the entire family. Major changes such as transitions in leadership lead to major problems. One brother being anointed by the father to become CEO, for example, creates an uproar among the other siblings and cousins. They are not happy, but they work hard. This is the Erickson family.

- **United and Industrious:** This is the ideal family business type. These people like to work, they like each other, and they are committed to the business and to the family. They enjoy the work and often have great ideas because there is room for real innovation and creativity within this type of system. They can withstand conflict and disagreement and, more importantly, are willing to find solutions. They are not interested in fighting that much. They are pretty happy, and they work hard. This is the Cleary family.

In our survey family, we have mixed results: they are industrious, they work hard, and they have been committed to one another.

But they are in crisis right now. At the present time, they would appear more divided and industrious, which may spell a change from a period when they were both united and industrious—or at least they have believed this about themselves.

Know yourself

If you are to make a successful transition, i.e., one that is not too damaging to anyone or the business, it is important to know as much about yourself, the family, and the business as possible. The knowledge you might gain from figuring out what type of family business you are, for example, can be invaluable to understanding what the next steps might be for you. For example, as the Clearys moved through the process, they paid close attention to the fact that there was a major change in the family—Mom's devastating illness. It is the type of change that touches everyone in the family and shakes families to their very roots. They also knew that since Dad wanted to step away from the business, take a less active role, and eventually hand over control and ownership to the kids, they needed to plan as best they could to make that work in a reasonable and smooth manner.

Since our focus here is on the development of the leaders for the family enterprise, we will walk through what the process was for Greg Cleary in particular, as he was to assume the senior leadership role in the company.

In our example, Greg became more involved in the local university family business center. Along with his siblings and dad, he participated in many of the offerings of the center, including the monthly breakfast meetings, which were topical in nature. There he listened to invited experts and other family business members. Along with these larger meetings, he joined the "NextGen group," which consisted of the members of the next generation in each family business who would assume or had assumed the president or CEO role. Greg found these contacts enormously helpful; he met these people during the other meetings, but he learned more about their businesses and their families from various social contacts. As a group they had a forum to explore what it actually meant to them as individuals to become the next in line, with all the issues surrounding that like stepping into some pretty big shoes and being the one who had to answer to Mom, Dad, siblings, and employees about the business. The issues of how one grows into a role, the process involved, and how to manage it all became part of their regular discussions.

The process of developing the next generation of leaders might look like this.

ASSESS   PLAN   ACT   REFLECT   RESET

1. Assess: Learn about you, the family, and the business.

Much of what Greg and the family did during this time was an assessment of themselves in each realm: as a family, as individuals, and as a business.

Many times assessments are more formal (a topic we will discuss at length later). For the Clearys, it was a less formal process, as they were all committed to moving ahead and getting it right the first time. The kids also began to see that as Mom declined Dad also became less involved in the business and even less interested in it. He seemed fine with the kids running things and assumed the role of senior adviser to their decision-making process.

2. Plan: Establish goals and how to achieve them.

Along with an assessment process is the planning process. This process, for Greg, involved his thinking about and consulting with advisers, Dad, and his brother and sister about what would be beneficial to his development as he moves toward becoming CEO. The outcome was a planning matrix that became the blueprint for his development. (This planning matrix is discussed in detail in subsequent chapters.)

- **What:** What is your goal? What are you working on? Be as specific as possible: "better time management; learn to communicate better; help other leaders be more accountable and self-reliant; or be more influential with the organization and more visible.

- **How:** How will you do this? "By reaching out to people I don't know well in the company; by going to meetings of other groups; and by working on better networking within and outside the company."

- **Resources:** What is it that you need to make this happen? "Get a coach who can help me; spend more time with Dad to find out how he ran the company; and take a course on management."

- **Deliverables:** "A progress report to shareholders every quarter." What is the time frame: "I will complete this in six months."

- **Success:** What does *success* mean in this context? Can it be measured?

3. Act: Implement the plan.

What resources do you need to be successful?

4. Reflect: How has this worked for you?

Do others see any difference? Can results be measured? What about this has worked? What needs to be tweaked or dropped? What have you learned about yourself in this process? How does this knowledge and understanding influence the way you lead the organization? Have you moved ahead?

5. Reset: What are the next steps?

Do you need another action plan? Do you need other resources—maybe more formal education, more knowledge about the industry, and more information about your products? Start with a blank sheet of paper and use the input from others.

What	How	When	Resources	Deliverables	Success
1.					
2.					
3.					

Figure 2-2: Development Planning Matrix

"What if I do nothing?"

This is always an option. Doing nothing actually means doing the same thing you have been doing. It may be avoiding making decisions, not planning, not communicating to others about transitions, or ignoring what's happening, also known as the *sticking your head in the sand approach*. Doing nothing is an option, but it's just not something that will lead to a good result. In this way, doing nothing means not creating the circumstances for success.

The Cleary family has many challenges, but they are determined to do something, even if they are not totally sure what that should be. They have made the decision to act. This is far more important than trying to get it absolutely right. That will never happen. Making the decision is the tough part. Figuring it out will happen, given some guidance, stick-to-itiveness, and a real desire to make it all work. In a family business this all adds up to commitment to the family and the business, and striving to be successful. It is no fun having a successful business when the family is fractured and the heart of the family is dying.

Bang and bucks

Determination and goodwill are wonderful things. Putting some money behind it is even better. None of this can happen without some expenditure. It is a business expense and should be viewed that way. The family getting involved in the business center and Greg getting some assistance are important for the business. This is not just fluff or "soft stuff" that has no business value. These efforts are always valuable for the business. As we will discuss later, recent years have brought more research evidence that leadership development activities, including executive coaching, have real, tangible results in the business. Keep this in mind.

Take the long view

At some point, the leadership development process takes a bit of trust that it is a good thing for everyone concerned. The millions spent by many large companies on these activities do not stem from goodwill but from strategic business decisions that these activities, over the long haul, will help keep key talent in the organization, keep them engaged, and prepare them for further roles and responsibilities. Have the long view about the business and the family.

⌘ ⌘ ⌘

Checklist

✓ Develop a strategic business plan.

✓ Include leadership development as part of that plan.

✓ Take a snapshot of what kind of family business you are.

✓ Talk to each other—a lot.

✓ Commit to developing your leaders.

✓ Don't freeze up and do nothing.

Three

Elegant Wheels

The Morelli family

In 1952, when Pietro and Christina Morelli steamed to the United States from their hometown, Modugno, Italy, they had many plans and aspirations. In Modugno, Pietro had started a baby carriage shop. He began handcrafting buggies and then larger carriages. His focus was on "building the best and nothing but the best," he said. In the United States, they started their family with Salvatore arriving first. They settled in Boston's North End, which had long been a welcoming venue to immigrants from Italy.

Pietro knew that he could never really work for anyone else for very long. He planned his move to leave his job and save enough money to rent a small factory space north of the city. In time, he made the move and began operations for *Bambino Carriage Company*. His skills as an artisan served him well as he used only the best materials: canvas from England, real rubber tires made to his specifications, and exotic woods from around the globe.[4]

The business grew, and the family grew. After Salvatore came Rosa and, finally, baby Guiseppina. All the children became test subjects for the newest models of the *Bambino* brand. The customer base grew, the reputation grew, and the business did well. The family became every immigrant's success story in their new land. They were proud and rightly so. The 1950s and 60s were good, but business started to slip in the 70s. Parents were not so willing to pay premium prices, even if the carriages were the best in the world. They retooled, extended their lines, and offered many more strollers than carriages. They stayed in business by recognizing the market and understanding they needed to adapt to the times.

---

4 Many thanks to Max Donnellan for his creative input about the *Bambino Carriage Company*.

The 90s were a boom time. They offered complete lines of strollers and carriages plus all of the accessories that parents now demanded.

And, the family changed. Salvatore, although having worked in the business as a teen and after college, lost interest in the business and attended law school. He became legal counsel for the business and the family. Rosa and Pina showed increased interest in the business, particularly after college, marriage, and starting their own families. They liked the work, liked the products, and were naturals when it came to business sense. With Dad at the helm and Mom spending more time with her charitable work in the city, the girls carved out their niches in the business.

In fact, Rosa saw the opportunity to compete with the *Angelina* brand of very high-end carriages. *Angelina* maintained their offices in Italy and imported to the United States and other countries through their satellite offices. They had grown heavy at the top and couldn't nimbly respond to market changes. Rosa calculated that they could offer an extraordinary product and undercut *Angelina's* top-of-the-line carriage, which retailed for well over $4,000. She calculated that because *Bambino* was an American product it had many advantages, not the least of which was that they did not have to pay the high import tariffs that *Angelina* did. She was right. They launched their "*Bambino CEO Supreme*" for under $3,000. It was a huge success in the high-end market.

The catalog captured the elegance of the *Supreme*:

> *Manufactured of imported inlaid woods and natural materials according to Bambino's old-world tradition. Tailored fabrication with attention to the smallest of detail. Individually crafted elegant and tactile chromium-plated hood compasses enable extraordinarily easy opening and closing. Paired chromium-plated side handles. Delicate organza curtain assures complete privacy. Sumptuous label with gold-leaf decorations. The ultimate in Bambino luxury. For the "Bambino who deserves the best."*

Pietro paid close attention to what the girls were doing and was very pleased. Rosa had a natural knack for recognizing opportunities, reading the market, and doing everything it took from R&D, design, manufacturing, and marketing to get the product out the door. As a $100 million company, they were growing at a good clip. Dad saw her potential.

Since Mom, Dad, and the three kids were the shareholders of the company, they would meet at the office and at home over long dinners with all the grandchildren and spouses in attendance. They discussed the growth of the company and how to make sure this would be an enduring legacy for the entire family. There was lots of pasta along with passion at their get-togethers. They cared deeply for one another and focused on how to continue to have a great family and a great business.

Dad felt comfortable with the girls and what they were doing. He didn't feel he needed to spend that much time at the business every day. In time, discussions would turn to thinking about transitions in the business and what Mom and Dad were considering as next steps for them. They talked of the house they bought back in Modugno and their desire to spend more time there and to travel more. They were both in good health and felt this was the time to do it, while they still could get around without needing their own senior version of the *"Bambino CEO Supreme."*

> In order for the next generation to be capable recipients of the knowledge of their seniors, preparations must begin in childhood. Opportunities that enable transmittal of the core values of the family and the firm must be created. Prospective successors must obtain appropriate education and practical experience in other organizations to build self-confidence. (F. Hoy and Sharma, "Entrepreneurial Governance in the Family Firm.")

As a family, they wanted to hold on to the balance between the business and the family they felt they had created in their lives. They turned their sights on how to manage the transition.

Like the Clearys, they did get involved with the family business center at the nearby university. The programs and relationships they developed there proved helpful. And it confirmed for them that they were on the right track in dealing with the issue of transition before it became a crisis, as it had become for the Erickson family.

Since there were so many areas to address, they realized they needed outside help and guidance. Although Salvatore was a good lawyer, he was not an expert on estate planning. He put Mom and Dad in touch with an estate-planning attorney. They needed to pull their financial planning into line and engaged a financial planning professional. They engaged a life insurance specialist as well, once they realized that needed to be a component of the estate plan. They developed a list of all the things they needed to address to make the transition. On the business side, it was also clear that they needed to develop a strategic plan for the next several years. The family business center proved helpful, as did a strategic planning consultant who helped them go through the process of developing a plan for the next five years.

On the family side, the legacy and values of the family were very important. They considered having a family council and a sibling group. A consultant helped Pietro and Christina craft a transition checklist of what they needed to pay attention to if they were to be successful in their efforts.

For Us	For the Family	For the Business	For Owners
• Complete an estate plan. • Create a plan for lifelong financial security • Get ready for the next chapter in our lives • Stay healthy	• Create a family mission statement • Ensure the family values are transmitted to each generation • Develop career paths for other family members	• Create a strategic plan • Choose a successor • Have a contingency plan for succession • Develop the top leadership	• Transfer ownership and control • Empower the team of owners • Craft a policy for family participation in the business • Create a board with outside directors

Figure 3-1: Transition Checklist

The checklist proved helpful because they could visualize and set dates for when they would complete each piece on the list. Although this may appear quite simple, in fact this process occurred over several years. But they stuck to it.

Who helped them?

The Trusted Adviser

- Most of us at one point or another in our lives have had a coach, teacher, or friend who helped us out. Often, a trusted adviser knows the family and the business well. This person (usually one) occupies an important place in the family business. He/she becomes confidante, guide, or sometimes maintains an operational role in the organization. This is an exceedingly important role and one that many who work with family businesses seek to occupy. The trusted adviser is viewed sometimes almost reverentially as the elder—the wise person who knows the family well. Sometimes this is a relative or the lawyer or accountant or financial adviser. This person's input into the mix is taken very seriously and carries great weight. In my own experience, this happens rarely. When, for example, members of a family business began calling me "Uncle Gerry," I knew that I had somehow gone from being another consultant to them to someone they really listened to.

  The Morellis relied on Uncle Tony, who had known them "forever." As a relative, he offered a perspective on family that only he could provide. Over time, the estate-planning attorney stepped into this role.

The family business adviser

- The family business adviser usually comes from some defined profession such as law, accounting, financial planning, psychology, or insurance. As an adviser, these individuals are hired by the firm for specific functions, depending on the profession. They are valued for their expertise and wise counsel to the family business. They may have knowledge of family dynamics or systems issues or have advanced training as is offered by the Family Firm Institute, an internationally known and highly regarded organization of family business advisers and consultants.

Generally, the focus of the adviser is on the result, be it an estate plan, financial plan, or addressing insurance needs. The Morellis assembled their advisory team early on in the process and required the advisers to communicate with one another regularly. They engaged a leadership development specialist to work with Pina and Rosa.

The family business consultant

- The family business consultant or family wealth consultant has a wider focus than the adviser. These consultants focus on helping the individuals and groups to work effectively as separate groups while being connected to the whole network of systems mentioned above: the business, the shareholders (the owners), and the family, and as an interconnected system. They will work with individuals (such as for leadership development), groups (the family business leadership teams), and the owners (with the board or the shareholders). Many are trained in the behavioral sciences such as psychology or social work, while others come from management consulting backgrounds or have been members of family businesses. Their focus is on the various systems of the family business and the business.

Consultants operate, many times, in more than one system in their work and may team up with other consultants or advisers to work in an interdisciplinary manner. They have been referred to as "process consultants." To be effective, they must offer a real business value. For example, in my work as an executive coach with senior leaders, the value I might bring is to help that person become more focused, less scattered, and more strategic in his/her approach. Ultimately, this work should have an impact on the business.

The family business system

- Every family enterprise consists of at least three groups: the family, owners, and the business.

- Each of these groups is made up of individuals.

- They act as a system, much like an automobile: each part of the car must be in tune with itself *and* with the rest of the car. A car will not run well if it has a malfunctioning electrical system or a clogged fuel line.

- The system may work well or not so well. Trouble in one part of the system affects all other parts of the system. For example, a great business easily can be run into the ground in one generation because of family discord, bitterness, resentment, or greed. It does not take much for the whole system to come crashing down.

The relationship of these groups to each other is captured in the *Three Circle Model* (Tagiuri, R., Davis, J.A. (1982). *Bivalent attributes of the family firm.* Working Paper, Harvard Business School, Cambridge, Massachusetts. Reprinted 1996, Family Business Review IX (2) 199-208.)

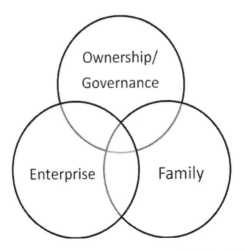

Figure 3-2: The Three Circle Model

How did this consultant help them?

The job of the consultant was to help both Rosa and Pina craft a development plan that would address their unique needs, given their respective roles in the company. Using a *Gap Analysis* approach, a tool to understand what one's goals and what skills one needs to achieve those goals, it was clear that Rosa had many talents and skills. She knew how to engage people on her team to be enthusiastic and energized in the work, she knew how to be firm when she necessary, and she grew up in business and knew it top to bottom. But she did need to focus on a few things.

Rosa's list:

- Finance.
- Talent Management: How to get the best people for the job.
- Management.

Pina needed to focus on:

- Learning more about marketing approaches and programs.
- How to develop the best sales and marketing team.
- How to manage those who reported to her.

With these goals in mind, they each worked on "how to get there from here." They detailed, along with the consultant, a plan involving a set of experiences such as formal courses workshops, reading, and working with the consultant on each of their goals. The three would meet regularly to discuss their program and chart their next moves. Pina and Rosa became very good at getting to the heart of the matter and figuring out what they needed to accomplish their goals.

What	How	When	Resources	Deliverables	Success
Finance	Exec. Ed. course	Spring	Time/Money	report	Understand the numbers better
Talent Development	HR Consultant	Now Twice per month	Time/Money	report	Better decisions
Management	MBA course	Summer	Time/Money	report	What management style works here

Figure 3-3: Rosa's Development Plan

With their plans posted on the wall in their offices, they were reminded each day of what they were working on and what they needed to be doing to achieve success.

Through this process, Rosa and Pina also learned about how best to use their consultant. They learned that good consultants know what their area of expertise is and what it is not. Part of the role of the consultant was to steer them in the right direction for what they needed, although this may not be the consultant's area of expertise. For example, it was evident that each woman had tremendous talent, ambition to succeed, and wanted this company to continue the family's legacy. Together they enrolled in an intensive university-based course for family business leaders. The course spanned a year with several on campus meetings, each lasting one week. In this course, they heard from leading experts on all aspects of family business, including many of the issues they faced in their own business. More than that, they connected with a cohort of members of other family businesses. They learned to support and challenge each other and learn from each other in their groups.

At the end of the course they were not only thrilled to have completed it, but felt they understood more about themselves, the business, and the family. The course allowed them to craft action steps that they implemented in the business.

A significant component of Rosa and Pina's development activity involved their relationship with Dad. One of the great gifts that the founding father or mother can bestow on the children is the gift of sharing knowledge, expertise, and, most importantly, passion for the enterprise. As part of their plan, the girls held regular meetings with Dad, separate from shareholder meetings or family meetings, to talk about the business, how he did it, what drove him, and what he understood about what worked and what didn't based on his experience. When discussing going head to head with *Angelina* and introducing *Bambino CEO Supreme,* he shared his thinking and reservations about doing it at all. He knew it was a huge investment and if they failed to pull it off, could prove disastrous for the firm. At the time, however, he spoke only about how to succeed, how fabulous that carriage needed to be, what a great idea it was, etc. "But in my heart," he said, "I knew this was a great risk, and it might not work at all. But I wanted Rosa to feel like I was really behind her, not just in words, but also in a real way. I am so relieved it worked!"

Such generosity and willingness to make way for the next generation can have long-lasting benefits for all involved. It freed Dad from the worry and anxiety about the business and gave him room to think about next steps with his wife. When this step is accomplished early enough in the process, Mom and Dad can feel that they are free to choose how they want to live their lives, while empowering the kids; the children bring their own creativity, energy, and innovation to the enterprise. It is energizing for all involved. Unfortunately, in too many situations this is where Mom and Dad are stuck. They can't quite cede that last bit of control to the next generation.

Getting stuck like this does happen, probably more often than not but with some guidance and good advice some families can move beyond it.

How does the consulting process work?

1. **Meetings**

    Everyone loves a good meeting—or maybe not. Usually when a suggestion is made to work with an outside consultant or adviser, the parties will meet to get a feel for each other—the chemistry meeting. But even before that, there is usually contact by phone. This is time to get some answers before going too far down the road. This is the time to ask:

    "Have you worked with family businesses long? What kinds of businesses? Can you give us an example? How do you think you might approach our situation? What are your fees compared to everyone else who does similar work?" The questions can go on, but you want to get a feel for this person and get some sense that this might be someone you might want to work with. Many times the stories and vignettes that the consultant can tell about families that he/she has worked with are very telling.

    In a family business, the decision to work with an outside professional is very significant. Many families feel like it is like "bringing someone into the family."

    After the phone contact, the goal of the first meeting is to discuss the current situation and get some sense from the consultant about his or her approach and how he or she would work with you in this situation. Many of the questions above would be brought up.

    Where to meet? This often is a crucial question. Many consultants will come to your office (if there is enough room for a confidential conversation) or sometimes families prefer to meet over lunch at a restaurant. Other families prefer to meet in the home. Particularly if this meeting is just with Mom and Dad, the home many times is preferred.

2. **Contracts**

    Once there is a comfort level established, and you feel that this is someone that you could work with, the next issue is how to define the scope of the project/work. Some professionals work on an hourly basis, while others prefer a project-based arrangement. Whatever the approach, it should be something with which you are comfortable will work given your situation. Most people do not like to be "nickel and dimed to death," so it is important to understand what the range might be for the engagement on an annual basis. You need to plan to budget this into your business. This is a business expense, as it is for the betterment of the business. It is much cleaner and sensible to take this route, although in some circumstances clients prefer to keep it out of the business and off the books and some fund it personally.

3. **Work**

The scope of the work, timelines, billing, payment expectations, and other issues such as "extras" need to be spelled out. Many consultants bill for their travel time, if they are on an hourly fee schedule. If the travel is minimal, e.g., less than half an hour, many will not bill for this time. Whatever the situation, it should be spelled out clearly.

The important thing is the work. What the work is and who will be involved is critical. If, for example, the agreement is to have a series of meetings both with the family as a group and with individual family members and to devise a plan for the transition of the business, this should be laid out in the agreement. While being as specific as possible in your expectations is important, there also needs to be room for flexibility. Many consultants and advisers will outline several phases of the work, with room to renegotiate the timeline, as the process unfolds. There needs to be flexibility on both sides if the process is to be successful.

4. **Integration**

A key component in the work phase is the issue of integration of the new ways of doing things into the business and the family. For example, if the family realizes that they have a lot work to do in terms of communication with each other, there needs to be a time for the "new way" to be practiced and integrated into the old. The more specific action items the better. "We need to meet as a family once a month to talk about where we are in this process, how we are doing, and what we want to accomplish." Or, "Mom and Dad should have some discussion with each other about what they want to do and then come back to us in a month." Global statements such as, "We just need to talk to each other more," demand no accountability or further action from the participants. Specific is good.

5. **Moving on**

Over time, the boundaries and parameters of the work with the consultant/adviser become clearer and better defined. In many instances, what started out as a project to improve communication in the family, for example, moves into the business realm as the need for strategic planning becomes evident.

There is no need to be wedded to one outside professional for all your needs. There are many good professionals whose work is completely focused on strategic planning, while others do executive coaching or senior team development. The choice of the professionals really should fit the needs at that moment. Many families find that over the years they work with a range of professionals, advisers, and consultants, depending on the circumstances at the time.

Notes about consultants

- Consultants need to make money.

- They also want to help you make money and reach your goals.

- The best consultants are strategic and want to get the work done as efficiently as possible.

- Family business consultants and advisers need to have deep knowledge about families and about their businesses.

- Consulting is a process and not a onetime deal.

- Your consultants and advisers need to be clear with you about the contract, expectations, payment, and who does what.

What do we gain?

Many family businesses like to pinch their pennies. Generally, this might be a good thing. In the case of developing the next generation of leaders, it is not such a good thing. There are many challenging and difficult issues such as facing the reality that planning for transitions and developing leaders is all for the good of the business.

> **Use your advisers and consultants**
>
> These are professionals that you trust and rely on. They are there to offer guidance, support, and advice. Use them wisely.

The most difficult issue, of course, concerns facing one's own mortality. No matter what Pietro Morelli does, he will pass from this world. No one likes to face this, yet the fact remains. He can do the best thing for the family and the business by recognizing that fact and making some good decisions. Fortunately, he and Christina did make good decisions.

They avoided what is called the "Complacency spiral." This is the tendency to assume that all will remain the same, that the business will always do fine, and all will be good. It is easy to be lured into this kind of complacency, but it is extraordinarily dangerous to succumb to it. Certainly, we have witnessed profound examples of this with the recent recession. Complacency, arrogance, and greed do not mix well when stirred with the emotions generated in a family: the reaction is explosive and sometimes catastrophic. This spiral into complacency only ends in disaster.

> Given the pivotal position of a leader, much care and self-discipline is needed in selecting and preparing the next generation for leadership roles. (Hoy and Sharma, 2008)

So what do you gain? You should see a measure of success, happiness, and predictability in one's life and in the lives of those important to you.

Successful family businesses

One way of depicting all the moving parts to making a successful family business transition is the **Family Business Success Pyramid** (below). It is a variation of the hierarchy of needs popularized by Dr. Abraham Maslow. In this variation, the important issues related to fulfilling needs that are more basic are at the bottom of the pyramid. They serve as a foundation for fulfilling the needs above. Each level rests on the one below. Without attending to and dealing with more fundamental needs, a family business cannot fulfill its dream of being successful, viable for many generations, and remaining a cohesive family unit. This is the key to a successful transition from one generation to another.

The everyday, practical translation of the pyramid was Pietro's and Chrsitina's checklist. All of the "things to do" on that list fit into this pyramid. The pyramid is just another way of looking at what has to be done from a little wider vantage point. It is the "big picture."

Figure 3-4: Family Business Success Pyramid

The Morelli's Now

Christina and Pietro spend the New England winter months in Modugno. Pietro could not resist and opened a modest carriage shop/toy store. No high-end carriages, just what the local people can use. Rosa and Pina have been running the company for five years. They have had their bumps, but they have worked out the major kinks regarding roles and are quite pleased with the results. The company saw a downturn with the recession, but they have managed to hold on to all their employees. They are developing new lines for the next generation of parents. Salvatore, still very close to the family, pursued his dream and opened a ski and snowboarding shop in Vermont, close enough to attend all the big family events and holidays. He is also general counsel for one of the big ski resorts. There are now seven grandchildren all of whom, at one time or another, have spent some considerable time in a hand-me-down *Bambino CEO Supreme*—no entitled bambinos, just regular kids.

⌘   ⌘   ⌘

Checklist

✓ Do something to develop the next generation. Get started.

✓ Choose advisers and consultants based on what your goals are.

✓ Involve the family in the process.

✓ Take the "big picture" view of the transition. It will take time.

✓ Understand and nurture your core family values.

✓ Don't fall into the "Complacency Spiral."

✓ Anything you do will cost a few bucks. Chill. It is all worth it *and* is much cheaper than losing the company *or* your family.

Four

Creating Sparks

The Sparks family

When Roy Sparks returned home from World War II, he didn't have any plans for work. He had worked briefly in his Uncle Harry's mattress store after high school. He knew he had to do something fast as all the returning vets would be looking for work. He and Dolores, his high school sweetheart, had married shortly before he had shipped out in 1942. He had missed her terribly, especially since the arrival of little baby Eddie in 1943. Eddie and Dolores were the joys of his life. As he considered his options, he wondered if maybe Uncle Harry would take him back, at least temporarily.

Harry did take him back, and he began working at the *Sparks New and Used Mattress* store. It was in a good location in downtown, and with all the growing families, he knew business would be good. Uncle Harry and Aunt Tess did not have kids of their own, so Roy had a special place at their table and in their home. He enjoyed the work, and business was good, so that eventually he and Dolores were able to get a little place of their own and move out of the apartment near the store. Their little family grew as Ruth and Ann were born.

Roy stayed with his uncle, and as time passed, Harry began to talk to Eddie about taking over the store. They had no written agreements, only their handshake. Eddie took over the business, and he was able to provide for Harry and Tess in their later years.

Sparks Mattress soon became the leading mattress retail outlet in the region, with several stores and more opening each year. In time, Eddie expanded operations and decided to get into the manufacturing side of the business; he acquired his primary manufacturer. This acquisition proved fortunate because it allowed him to run everything from manufacturing to distribution to sales. He began selling to department stores around the country and soon had a business that thrived through all the ups and downs of the economy.

Eddie joined his father in the business after college. He had always liked being in the store and found it fun to be selling to customers, especially when he could get them to spring for one model higher than the one they had planned to buy. He married Marie in 1969. His sisters, Ruth and Ann, did not have much interest in the business, although they would help out sometimes when the business was growing. Besides, they were busy with their own young families.

Eddie and Marie's fist son, Corey, was born in 1970. The whole family was thrilled with the first grandchild. Brad came along in 1973. He had Down's syndrome and required care because of his significant limitations and heart problems. Eddie and Marie adjusted their lives. When Stan was born in 1978, they had the knowledge and perspective of more mature parents and made room for another boy in the home.

The Sparks family genogram

The diagram below is called a *genogram*. A genogram is used to map the history of the family in a way that is different from a family tree. In a family business setting it is used to show the relationships of the all of the members to each other and to keep track of the business changes. In the Sparks family genogram, which shows three generations, the third generation of Corey, Bradford, and Stan are at the bottom, while the top shows Roy and Dolores who were married in 1942. The black square in Bradford's box indicates intellectual or mental disability. There are many other symbols and indicators that can be added to a genogram, some for example, showing dysfunctional relationships, divorces, deaths, etc. The Sparks Family genogram illustrates how one might show the family tree in a more dynamic way that captures something of the progression of the generations and their relationships.

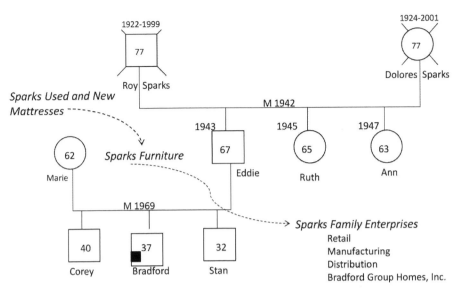

Figure 4-1: Sparks Family Genogram

Eddie grows the business

Under Eddie's leadership, the business did well. They had expanded, and, particularly since the arrival of Bradford, Eddie and Marie were more aware of the needs of the disabled and those with limitations or illness. They acquired a hospital bed manufacturer and opened several retail stores selling the beds along with other home-care equipment. This addition, although a small part of the company, became very important to them as a family as they wanted to pay attention to the needs of people less fortunate than themselves.

Corey joined his father in the business shortly after college and, like his father, was a natural, with a knack for operations, planning, and running the stores.

In 1995, Eddie made a strategic decision about the business that changed everything. He came to realize that he could not do everything and that he was not good at some things. He knew he was great at being the "face of *Sparks Furniture*," as it was now known. He also came to see that he did not like the day-to-day operational details of running the business. He knew he needed help. He brought in Frank Stone to run operations. He had known Frank from the industry. He also knew Frank had been looking for another opportunity. Frank took the position, with the agreement that within two years, if he did well, he would be named CEO. Eddie had a hard time with this agreement, but ultimately gave in because he thought Frank could bring something to the company that he could never provide—the vision and extraordinary financial acumen to grow it.

In the years since Frank Stone assumed the position as CEO, *Sparks Furniture* exceeded all expectations and broke the $100 million mark in sales. They acquired competitors and formed several divisions, all linked under *Sparks Family Enterprises*. Young Stan joined the business within a couple of years after college, after having spent some time in other retail and manufacturing companies. With the addition of Stan to the family enterprise, the pieces seemed to all fit into place.

This close family had long been involved in organizations for the mentally and physically disabled. They felt that they had reached a position that they actually might be able to do something tangible and real for these people, including their own son, Brad. They opened *Bradford House* in 2005. This was first of many group homes for those with physical and mental challenges that the family opened in the years that followed. It was the Sparks family at their best—helping those less fortunate and offering something that was sorely needed in the area. Brad, himself, now a young man, enjoyed the fact that he could be on his own, be in a supervised setting, and develop a life separate from his family. It seemed to work well for everyone.

In the last two years, Eddie and Marie began thinking about and planning for their own retirement and the next steps in their lives. They felt that the business was going well with Frank Stone at the helm, that Brad was being cared for, and that Corey and Stan were now integrated into the business. The big question, among many they faced, was how to plan for the continuity of the enterprise as a family business. Frank was making noises about the need to do this, as he was not "going to be around forever."

In a shareholders meeting Eddie and Marie announced to the family that they had decided on a plan for the transfer of the business. In the plan, Corey would assume the CEO position in three to five years. During that time, he would work with Frank to learn more about the business and the role that Frank played; Corey also would immerse himself in a development plan for himself as he prepared to take over leadership of the company. It was left unclear what role Stan would play in all of this. There was a lot of fallout from this meeting. Corey, although flattered to be chosen to succeed Frank, felt that this was a daunting task and maybe he would never measure up to Frank, the revered and extraordinarily competent leader of the family enterprise. The idea was actually Frank's as he felt that he needed to do something to move the process of the transition along; they had talked and talked for years about transition options.

Stan himself was dumbfounded and hurt because this succession plan seemed to come out of left field, with no real input from him, Corey, or anyone else. He had only been with the firm a couple of years and still was feeling his way into his job. He was responsible for all of the group homes, which had grown over the years to include thirteen in the area. His budget continued to grow, and he still struggled to make a profit in a very tight market, with many reimbursements coming from insurance and state programs. It was a tough job. He was left feeling deflated and unsure of himself, and began to wonder if he really wanted to be in the business with the family.

Within a year of this announcement Eddie and Marie, with Frank Stone's input, decided that maybe they should consult a family business adviser. They began working with Dave Schwartz. As part of the assessment process, Dave interviewed all of the family members, including Brad. He reported back to the family and recommended several things, among them:

- Expand the board of advisers to include outside members, as well as family shareholders.

- Work with Corey to craft a development plan as he moved toward his new role as CEO.

- Work with Stan on how he might address the issues within his own business and help him think through his own career objectives

- Work with the family to establish family governance groups, such as a family council and a sibling group.

- Work with Eddie and Marie to plan their transition, particularly regarding transferring ownership of this very complicated, interconnected family enterprise.

- Consult with Frank Stone about his timetable and plans for leaving his leadership role.

Work with Stan

Since Dave Schwartz would be working closely with Corey on his development for moving into the CEO role, he suggested that Stan work with another adviser who specialized in executive coaching and career development. Although Stan initially balked at the idea, he soon came to see some value in trying it. Since he had felt burned by the sudden decision to name his brother to the top leadership role, he was leery of this possible work with an adviser and had many questions.

He met with Bill Jorgenson, the adviser. He asked about his qualifications, if he worked with family businesses, his connection to the other adviser, whether what he said would be considered confidential, etc. It was important, given the circumstances, that the issue of confidentiality and trust be put on the table immediately. He asked Bill, "Are you just here to ease me out the door?" Bill, a seasoned adviser and psychologist, replied that the relationship was confidential and based on trust, and that, no, he was not there to "ease him out the door." He told Stan that he would need to coordinate with the other advisers involved with the family and that he would want to talk with Frank periodically.

Executive coaching

Bill then outlined the process and what coaching is, compared to other forms of individual work with clients in a family business.

He explained that his focus was on Stan and his role as a business leader. He explained that executive coaching:

- Is an individual activity that occurs between the executive and his or her coach.

- Is designed to improve the effectiveness of the leader in producing business results.

- Is informed by feedback and data from the coach and the executive's organization.

- Invites the executive to reflect on and learn from his or her own experience, and to practice new ways of thinking and behaving that produce more effective outcomes

- Teaches the executive tools to continue learning after formal coaching has ended.[5]

He also explained that coaching was not counseling or psychotherapy and was not a substitute for therapeutic work, as sometimes there is the perception that coaching is "therapy for executives." He wanted to make clear to Stan that their work together was a partnership that took into account all these elements. This emphasis on business results was important to distinguish their work from other forms of coaching or consulting. There were business issues that needed to be addressed, including staffing concerns, going over the budget, and developing a cohesive team.

Much of this focus is captured in this definition of executive coaching:

> Executive coaching is an experiential, individualized, leadership development process that builds a leader's capability to achieve short and long-term organizational goals. It is conducted through one-on-one interactions, driven by data from multiple perspectives, and based on mutual trust and respect. The organization, an executive,

---

5 Thanks to Dr. Lew Stern for all of his thoughtful work on executive coaching.

and the executive coach work in partnership to achieve maximum learning and impact." [6]

What sets executive coaching apart from many other approaches is the emphasis on not only business outcomes but also the use of a comprehensive plan that includes assessment at the beginning. Usually the coach and the client agree to a formal contract that outlines ground rules, time frames, goals, and specific measures of success. It is not an open-ended process. In Stan's case, the coaching was *developmental,* i.e., focused on growth and change, as opposed to fixing something that had broken.

It is also a process of learning, with an emphasis on helping the coachee (the person being coached) understand and own his or her own style of learning. This approach usually involves:

- Tactical problem solving,

- Developing leadership capabilities and new ways of thinking and behaving that carry over to other situations, and

- "Learning how to learn": developing skills and habits of self-reflection that ensure that learning will continue after coaching ends.

Is this a good way to develop leaders?

This is always a good question. Sometimes the hiring of a coach is not appropriate for the situation. Some situations *do not* lend themselves to coaching and require something else. The limitations of coaching in family business include:

- Using a coach to deal with a spoiled relative with a sense of entitlement who has no motivation to change or deal with issues.

- Using a coach to deal with significant mental health issues or addiction to alcohol or drugs

- Using a coach to repair a broken marriage.

---

6 *The Executive Coaching Handbook* (4th Ed.) Online at:
www.theexecutivecoachingforum.com.

- Using a coach to address what is primarily a business issue.

- Using a coach as a replacement for dealing with family issues.

Hiring a coach is one part of a development plan. It can be tremendously helpful in situations like Stan's, where he needed to figure out what his next steps in his career might be, how he might develop within the business, and what he needed to do *right now* to be successful in his business. The decision to use a coach or not should rest on whether it makes good business sense, if it will be helpful to the business in the long run, and if the executive is someone the business should be investing in to develop as a leader. *It is not* a good use of coaching, in family businesses in particular, to be trying to remediate serious personality or mental health issues or very poor family dynamics.

The coaching process

In working with Stan, Bill laid out the process, so that Stan could understand how the process worked and the thinking behind each step.

1. **Assessment**

   The assessment process may involve any number and type of instruments or interviews to gather data. In Stan's case the assessment phase involved several different approaches:

Steps in the Coaching Process

1. Assessment

2. Feedback

3. Focus on real-time issues

4. Practice

5. Continued feedback

6. Monitoring the process: setting new goals

7. Transition to long-term development

   o Interviews:

     ▪ Biographical Interview: This gathers information about work history, family history, and history of the family enterprise.

     ▪ Behavioral Event Interview: This is an interview-based tool for garnering information about challenges and successes in work life.

o <u>Formal/Objective Testing</u>: There are scores of different personality tests and other kinds of psychological tests available. In Stan's case a set of tests was utilized to gather a wide range of information about areas of strength and weakness in his functioning at work.

- <u>Personality Profiles</u>: Two different personality profiles were used. Each one assessed specific behaviors correlated to work success. These profiles were used to determine what are Stan's strengths and how do they show up in a work situation? These tests are most appropriate for executives and senior managers

- <u>Risk Factors Survey</u>: This tool was used to assess how Stan performed under pressure. This is aimed at answering the question "How does Stan perform under pressure, and, under extreme circumstances, what are the possible derailers of his success?"

- <u>Vocational Interest</u>: This tool was used to capture Stan's career interests, capabilities, and skills. It was aimed at answering the question "What is Stan really interested in, where do his interests lie, and is his current position a good fit for him?"

- <u>Test of Critical Thinking</u>: This was a test somewhat like an intelligence test and was aimed at determining what are Stan's strengths in solving and dealing with complex problems and is he a good problem solver?"

Bill Jorgenson met with Stan and interviewed him for several hours. The remainder of the tests/surveys was taken online at a time of Stan's choosing. Many testing procedures are now conducted this way because it gives the person greater freedom to complete the assessment at his or her convenience.

Stan's assessment did not include a multirater (360-degree) survey. This type of survey gathers data from multiple individuals who know the person, including colleagues, direct reports, and supervisors. The purpose of this type of survey is to gain as complete a picture as possible of the person. This was not part of the assessment because of the sensitive nature of the work in this situation. Usually, this is an important piece of the puzzle. Bill did interview the CEO, Frank Stone, and Dave Schwartz, the family's trusted adviser.

2. **Feedback**

   From the data gathered, Bill Jorgenson wrote a report for Stan that covered the major areas of the testing. Here are some samples from the report:

   o <u>Key Strengths</u> (Current behaviors linked to business success)

   - Open to change
   - Eager for challenges
   - Flexible, imaginative approach to problem solving
   - Adaptable to changing environment
   - Independent, self-reliant
   - Bold and adventurous
   - Action oriented
   - Takes charge
   - Supports staff
   - Not risk-averse
   - Delegates well

   o <u>Development Need Areas</u> (To focus on and improve)

   - Planning
   - Influencing others
   - Attention to details
   - Sensitivity to criticism
   - Getting distracted and losing focus
   - Listening
   - Following through
   - Prioritizing

<u>Other feedback comments</u>:

"Stan is a person full of energy and always ready for action. This has served him well in his athletic pursuits through high school and college, and into the present. Indeed, in the athletic arena, he has always felt successful and willing to learn, demonstrating a talent for learning quickly. His success athletically has been a source of pride, contributing to his confidence and willingness to take risks. He has had the experience that risk taking and learning in the moment have served him well.

"Success in those areas contrasts with the educational arena, which has always been a source of frustration. Despite being a very bright person, he has had adequate but not stellar academic performance and a disinterest in formal classroom learning. He learns by observation, practice, and figuring things out in the moment. He likes to solve problems and prides himself on coming up with creative, innovative solutions.

"Since Stan is a self-reflective person, he is well aware of these challenges and, over the years, has devised strategies to overcome them. Although he cares little for learning from printed materials and "book learning," he listens and absorbs information accurately and retains it through that particular channel. His self-reflection has served him well. Rather than shying away from challenges, he seeks them out and is more than willing to put himself on the line in taking risks. His impatience and impetuousness, however, makes him jump a little too quickly at times, without regard for the consequences of not thinking through scenarios first.

"He is both a risk taker and adventurous, which can be a winning combination for the entrepreneur or those involved in a fast-paced business. With the mundane details of a more mature business, however, he is easily bored with details and planning. This boredom and frustration contribute to his difficulties with follow-though, planning, and attention to details. He can be visionary and have some great ideas, for example, to grow the business or in seeking out new deals. But the big-picture thinking does not translate well to the day-to-day conduct of the business.

"Although he thrives on the excitement and the hustle and bustle of a fast-paced environment, this sometimes gets in the way of actually getting the work done.

"With his need for independence and self-reliance, others may sometimes interpret this as arrogance and entitlement. Although Stan does not view himself as arrogant or entitled, this may represent a disconnect between his own self-perception and the perceptions of others."

Since there was a wealth of data from this assessment, the discussion between Stan and Bill offered an opportunity to get specific and detailed about what the next steps and goals might be. This collaborative partnership between Stan and Bill lasted throughout the entire engagement.

3. **Focus on real-time issues**

In working with Bill, Stan laid out this plan in separate buckets. Each bucket represented a major area that he needed to address. The strategy was to address each issue in each bucket over time, about six to nine months. During that time Stan would work on how to address the issue and then would practice it until he and Bill agreed that the issue was addressed. They agreed to meet every two weeks during this time and that they would talk about the day-to-day issues that Stan was dealing with. Periodically, they would also go back to the buckets and check where they were in the process.

⌘ ⌘ ⌘

Stan's Buckets

Career/Future Development

- Big picture: real passion and abilities/skills
- Leveraging strengths
- Where in three to five years?

Business/Management

- Manager: what to do?
- Use of assistant: getting clear
- Run better meetings
- Team development

Personal

- Frustration with role in the business
- Organization/focus issues: develop strategies
- Listening and thinking through: slow down that brain!

Family Business (With Dave Schwartz)

- Working with Dave Schwartz and family to identify, work through, and resolve family issues
- Gain perspective/education on issues of family and how they affect functioning in the business

⌘ ⌘ ⌘

Some of these issues were straightforward. For example, Stan wasted a lot of time in trying to get organized each day and would get sidetracked into areas that were not top priorities. Bill suggested making better use of his assistant, Sandra. She and Stan worked out a system so that each day, before Sandra would leave for the day, she would sit down with Stan and go over his schedule. They would see what he hadn't been able to get to that day and then plan the next day and the week. With this system in place, Stan made much better use of his time, was not sidetracked so much, and generally was much more productive.

Another issue was not so easy. One of the major concerns was the amount of staff overtime each week. There was too much, and it was busting the budget in that area every month. Since this was the largest budgeted category, it had to be brought under control. The supervisor in charge of this area, although well respected and well regarded as a professional, was not accustomed to staying within a budget, and reining in expenses. Stan expected this to be a very stormy process to deal with her and pull in the overtime. His approach was to sit down and go through the budget, look at where and when this was happening, and make it her responsibility to bring it into line.

They key to the work with her was to make sure she understood that the effect of this one budget item was enormous and was causing them to run in the red every month. Much of the work with her was focused on educating her about the budget process, and why it was so important to attend to this as a manager. His approach was not confrontational and more like one professional talking with another about an issue they would work on together. Within two months the budget and overtime was brought under control. The net result was that now she took full responsibility for her group and had a complete understanding of the process and the constraints on the budget. The business moved into the black and gradually began making more money.

In this arena, Stan demonstrated his significant skills at enlisting someone as a genuine ally and partner in the organization. It became a learning moment for all other members of this team, who saw how it worked and why it was so important. Another result was that the team itself became more cohesive and productive because of this experience. Stan also learned that he could trust his own judgment and instinct about how to best work with someone, as the result was right there in the bottom line.

4. **Practice**

Stan and Bill agreed that *Practice makes perfect* when it comes to changing behaviors that were unproductive. For example, during meetings Stan would sometimes get caught in the trap of trying too hard. The plan was to lay out the agenda, distribute it well in advance, and insist that, since there was only a certain amount of time to devote to each item and the meeting as a whole, it was important to be on time and ready to go. Within two meetings, everyone showed up on time, and meetings became much more productive: each person felt that his or her time was valuable, and he or she was there to get the work done and move on.

As part of the process of focusing on running the meetings and developing the senior team, Bill conducted an online survey of the team to get feedback for Stan and take the pulse of the team. Bill then attended the next team meeting and presented the results of the survey. Since the survey was focused on organizational issues and did not single out Stan per se, they could all address the major issues that came up from an organizational perspective. This discussion of the survey also resulted in better engagement by the team in their meetings. They focused on the top issues that they had identified.

5. **Continued feedback**

The meetings between Stan and Bill were most productive when Stan would come away with a deeper understanding of his behavior and how it might be affecting some issue with which he was dealing. For example, when Frank asked him to lead a core marketing group that had for some time been unfocused, Stan knew he had an opportunity to make an impact and at the same time prove himself to Frank. To him, this was not just another assignment. He could demonstrate how he was changing, by making this a more productive group. His approach to the group was to shift things so that they could feel that their ideas were not only respected but also valued. This shift in outlook by the members of the group, because of Stan's approach with them, was remarkable. They came up with great ideas about how they could move ahead. Stan remained the person to coordinate the group, without too much control. With this shift, the marketing efforts were more laser like in focus and had a better payoff down the road.

The learning for Stan was to see the change in the marketing group. It was clear to him (and to Frank) that his efforts had paid off. Stan discovered that he was adept at helping a group move forward and that this was one of his major personal assets that he brought to the family enterprise. He could feel very good about himself.

6. <u>**Monitoring the process: setting new goals**</u>

As Stan and Bill moved through the coaching process, they became partners in the work, and each felt that he was contributing to Stan's success, which made it that much easier to address more difficult issues. This joint problem-solving process allowed them to deal with a wide range of issues, from management problems to how to fire someone when necessary.

As part of the regular agenda in most meetings, they would check in, take a look at the goals and their progress, and make adjustments if need be. At one point, about ten months into the process, it was clear they needed to take a fresh look at the plan they had put in place months before. From that discussion, they crafted a new, streamlined plan with just three main goals (see figure 4-2 below). The goals were:

o Improve operational knowledge

o Improve influence

o Be more visible to the entire company

With these three goals, they then worked backward to specify what behaviors Stan would need to focus on to be successful. For example, if Stan wanted to improve his influence in the company as a whole (not just the group homes) he needed to:

o Be aware that he actually did have influence and act accordingly

o Work with Frank to understand where he might best develop that influence

In this revised plan, the goals and how to achieve them appeared simple and straightforward. In fact, these were not so easily achieved, as the goals were wider in scope than the previous goals.

In wanting to deepen his operational knowledge, for example, this meant literally getting to know people he did not know before, going to departments where employees had no idea who he was, and most importantly, asking lots of questions everywhere. Stan discovered that everyone loves to talk about what he or she does, especially when someone with authority (and the name on the door) is asking. One added benefit of all this effort was that, as he became more knowledgeable about the company, Stan could offer suggestions and perspectives to his brother Corey and to Frank as well. Clearly the entire organization benefitted from his hard work.

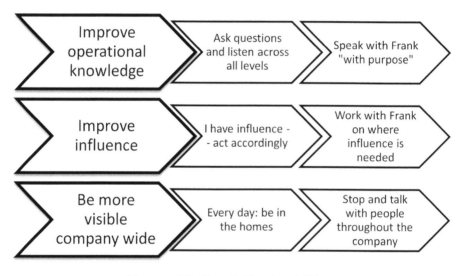

Figure 4-2: Stan's Revised Plan

Stan's plan reads from left to right. On the left is what Stan will do and on the far right is the goal to be achieved. With this revision, he was more focused on specific goals and how he would achieve them.

7. <u>Transition to long-term development</u>

The overall goal of the coaching process is to enable the individual to understand and develop his or her own learning style.

With maturity, experience, and leadership development activities like executive coaching, the individual should take ownership of his or her own development and seek out those experiences that will help him or her grow as leaders. Sometimes this may involve getting assistance with presentation skills because individuals are more likely to be spending some time doing presentations either inside or outside the organization when they move up the corporate ladder.

This transition may take some time, particularly if the coaching experience has been a truly beneficial one, in which the person feels that he or she has grown. Stan is in the midst of this transition. At the beginning of the work with Bill, Stan said, "I know this is a long-term process, and I am fine with that. I plan on having you in my life for a long time." This was not idle chatter, as Stan not only understood the importance of these kinds of helping relationships but also valued them tremendously. He knew, for example, that if he listened to his college coach, he would not only improve but would gain greater confidence in his abilities, since he would understand not only the body mechanics behind kicking the ball for accuracy and power, but what kind of mindset he needed to score goals.

Such a positive and engaged attitude on Stan's part did wonders for his progression in the work with Bill. Rather than becoming defensive about something he needed to work on, he would see it as a challenge to be solved and worked on. His competitive nature kicked in, as he wanted to be successful not only in the business but in the coaching with Bill.

Over time, Stan saw that not only did his piece of the family business get into the black, but it also made a very healthy profit to boot. All of these pieces together not only bolstered Stan's confidence, drive, and initiative but made it clear to all around him that he could be focused on business results and, at the same time, have a productive, engaged team. It was a win-win situation all around.

Why a coach? How about a couch?

One of the questions often heard about coaching is "Shouldn't these people just be in psychotherapy or counseling? Aren't these really mental health issues?" In Stan's case, for example, the issues were clearly leadership and business issues. Surely, there is an overlap with personal motivations and personality. However, in a developmental coaching process, as was true with Stan, the issues were framed and understood in a leadership growth model: he needed to learn more about being the kind of leader who can be successful in *that* organization.

There are situations that are well known to many family business owners and their families in which a particular person has significant mental health problems that need attention. Such issues demand attention not only for that person's health but for the good of the business as well. Families often are faced with family members who are addicted to drugs or alcohol. Most times, these issues *do* affect the business. Not being able to make it to the office on a Monday morning because a person is hung over is both a real business issue and a mental health issue. These issues must be actively and forcefully dealt with, if *both* the family and the business are ever to regain solid footing and prosper.

In such situations, the mental health issue must be faced head on before any coaching can be helpful. It can be extremely difficult for a family to come to grips with the fact little brother Tommy must deal with a significant addiction before he can be of any good to the business. Unfortunately, some families cannot bring themselves to either confront Tommy or find the resources to get him help. Many families will put up with enormous disruption and uproar from that person and still find no way to help him. They become trapped and hopeless about what to do.

This checklist may be helpful in these situations:

- How disruptive is this behavior to business? Is it interfering with the business? Are sales lost because of the behavior?
- How is this impacting the person's life? Loss of relationships with one's children or spouse can result.

- Is this a life-threatening emergency? Do family members spend too much of their time worried about that person, to the point that other matters fall by the wayside?

- Would another business, a nonfamily business, or a public company put up with this behavior?

- What are the consequences of doing nothing?

There are always consequences for doing nothing: the behavior worsens or becomes more dangerous, customers complain, sales are lost, or the business suffers in some other way. Many times families are adept at making excuses for their son or daughter or cousin or uncle. A typical scenario involves a family member who works in the business and treats employees poorly. A family member who gets away with and has no consequences for unruly behavior such as yelling at employees or being abusive is clearly destructive to the family and the business. Employees know full well that Tommy is getting away with something that they themselves would not get away with. This cannot be tolerated.

The issue, then, is the very *lack of consequences* for such behavior. Such behavior, if tolerated, is guaranteed to worsen. Tommy has no reason to improve since he faces no consequences. In other, nonfamily businesses, employees are put on a short leash, given a plan they must follow, with a time line, or face losing the job.

Is coaching just a fad?

Coaching, in one form or another, has been in the business world for many years. Before it became formalized in the last several years, there was always the close relationship an executive might have with a mentor, friend, or colleague whom the person could use as a sounding board. In these more formalized times for coaching, the process has become clearer and somewhat institutionalized.

With this institutionalization of the coaching relationship, there are certificate programs and formal training programs to train coaches. Some of these are good and some are not so good. There are several considerations to be taken into account before hiring a coach:

- Does this person have training as a coach? If so, what kind?
- Does he or she have significant experience in the business world, either as a consultant or as an employee?
- What are his or her references?
- At what level does the individual have significant experience as a coach? Has he or she coached only midlevel supervisors and not C-suite leaders?
- How long has he or she been doing this?
- Does he or she have training or a certificate in family business consulting?

This is a significant decision, and one that involves time and money. It should not be entered into lightly. Executive coaching can be enormously helpful in family businesses, if it is tied to the business goals and the overall goals for the success and longevity of the business as a family business.

Big Bang of coaching

Coaching, as a leadership development activity, can have enormous impact for three reasons:

- It is individually tailored.

Coaching is essentially an individually tailored adult learning program. It is like taking a private tutorial with an expert. As such, it can move along quickly, as the instructor is an expert and activities are geared to where the coachee needs to develop, without getting sidetracked on extraneous subjects. For example, if one of the issues with Stan had been to help him "find himself" as a leader (in an authentic way), then the goals and activities would be tailored to that end. In fact, since Stan was relatively young to be in such a position in the company, he did need to figure out who he was as a leader, what were his own values and beliefs about being a leader, and what really appealed to him about being a leader. In his work with Bill, all of these issues came to the fore and were part of the fabric of many conversations. Such conversations helped him sort through who he wanted to be as leader, in his own style and way of doing things.

- <u>It is focused on goals.</u>

Coaching is always tied to business goals. Stan needed to develop his own leadership style because he needed to be more successful in the business. His lack of organization, for example, did impact the business because he would get sidetracked in the course of a day and not accomplish what needed to be done. His difficulty in confronting the supervisor did have real consequences in the business: he was losing money every month it went on. What he needed to change was real and important for him *and* the business.

- <u>It is time limited.</u>

It is important to have time limits on the engagement. Many times, in a successful engagement, the work can continue for more than a year or two. Over time, there are less frequent meetings, perhaps once a quarter to check-in and review or to reengage when the person is promoted or has a significant challenge with which he or she is dealing.

Generally, artificial constraints *do not work*. "You get six sessions because that's all we can afford." Many times, the real issue is not so much how much it costs, as much as the resentment at spending anything at all. Clearly, smaller family businesses will have greater monetary constraints. Most companies, in terms of size, need to be at the level where they can consider leadership development as part of growing the business and something in which they are invested.

Keys to Growing Outstanding Leaders

- Over time
- In depth
- With focus

Where coaching fits in

As we have noted previously, coaching is one leadership development activity among many that should be considered. Just as taking one course in math does not make you a mathematician, so too, one activity to develop your leadership potential will not make you an inspiring leader. The key seems to be undertaking these activities over time, in a focused way, and in-depth. Attending seminars, taking a course, or doing some coaching or anything else, in itself, will never be enough to help someone grow as a leader. The support of the organization, both financial and otherwise, is extremely important. For Stan, this meant that the organization supported his coaching, paid for it, and the family and Frank all thought this was great idea. Such support is extremely important and cannot be underestimated.

⌘ ⌘ ⌘

Checklist

✓ Be transparent in planning—no surprises.

✓ Use a qualified, seasoned coach.

✓ Make sure the coaching is tied to real business issues.

✓ Review and adjust plans as needed.

Five

Welcome to Our Table

Dreams and expectations

We all have dreams and fantasies about our lives and the lives of those around us. We tend to think about our own lives and those immediately around us: our children, loved ones, and parents. Families in business together have an especially difficult time separating their own dreams from what might be good for the business or for the relatives involved in the enterprise. Our own wishes for our children, for example, sometimes blur with what *they* might want for themselves. In average families, this normal developmental issue is worked out somehow, either by the child going off on her own or by making it clear that she has her own desires about her life.

Whether we grew up in a large family, a small family, a blended or adoptive family or in no family at all, we all have internal pictures, or *templates*, of what the family is supposed to be like. Of course, then we have the reality of our own family. Usually there is a bit of a discrepancy and sometimes, a huge discrepancy.

We carry around these patterns or templates inside us. Sometimes we vocalize them, when as kids we might say, "I wish I had Johnny's mother. She is so nice, and she makes pancakes for breakfast, even

Family culture evolves from the establishment of patterns around major emotional issues such as closeness and separation, independence, and submission and dominance. These patterns give rise to rules and organizing principles. They are automatic and unquestioned. When families also work together in business, the patterns that have been developed over time around these major emotional issues are passed down and played out in the arena of the family business. (Hollander and Bukowitz, p. 140) during the week!" At other times, we are unaware of them and their influence on us. It is at those times when we are least aware of these unseen influences that we are likely to get into trouble. These internal scenes are played out in the family business. For example, Dad may expect that Mary will step into the leadership role because she has the education, the drive, the experience, and seems to want to do it. Yet, Mary may have a completely different perspective on the situation. She may feel that, although she loves the business, she really wants to get on with her own life, apart from the family. She may want to strike out on her own, create her own life, and build her own future.

With expectations, fantasies, dreams, and desires on both sides, there is bound to be a clash. This is where the term "lack of communication" seems appropriate. If Mary and her dad could find a way to have a conversation about what they expect from each other or their hopes for the future, they might not get into such a bind down the road. For many families who work together, this is where they seem to get into trouble. With expectations on both sides that are not discussed, the illusion is created that "We will just go on, Mary will lead the business someday, and everything will be great."

This is mostly a situation of two reasonable, generally rational people who just may not have talked enough. Although the conversations might be difficult, they are not impossible nor do they necessarily lead to such disharmony that the family (and maybe the business) fractures. Often, it is the *fear itself* of poor outcomes that keeps people frozen in their tracks.

At the extreme, there are the families in which the issue is beyond problems in communication. These are the families in which there is a dynamic, usually of long-standing duration, that leads to a massive, catastrophic failure of the family and its business. The Redstone family, for example, has been in the news for many years about the passing of the baton to the next generation (or maybe using it on them).

> The family has been feuding for many years.
> In a recent installment, Sumner Redstone,

the patriarch, now in his mid-eighties, has triumphed in the courtroom. As head of *National Amusements*, a company that has movie theaters and other interests in the U.S. and abroad, he believes the company might sell for close to $1 billion.

He has been feuding with his children, Shari and Brent, for years. Shari, who was set to take over the company, saw that dream go up in smoke when her father retracted that offer in 2007. She may never lead the company. They have cut off communication.

In the latest boil-up, Sumner's nephew, Michael Redstone, claimed he was owed millions of dollars by the family business after a share sale in 1984. However, after a trial, which saw Sumner, Michael and various other family members testify, the court ruled against Michael and in favor of Sumner. (*Campden Family Business Newsletter*, December, 2009.)

What makes people act this way? Certainly some of it is about money, as the stakes are significant. However, we all assume that most members of the senior generation of families want "harmony" in the family. They want their kids to get along, for everyone to enjoy their lives, and get together for holidays.

We could dismiss this behavior as a fluke, except that it happens all the time in family businesses. Most times one person cannot be blamed. Scapegoating a family member for causing the hubbub does occur. The answer is in the dynamics that have been operating in the family. These are not only the psychological dynamics of the relationships of the members with each other, but also the dynamics at play in the structure of the business and the governance structure.

As we discussed in chapter 2, there are several possibilities of "types" of family businesses (see figure 2-1). As we consider the Redstone family, the lower left quadrant of the illustration identifies these kinds of families as "divided and dependent." A family business can last quite a long time when the family falls in this quadrant, as long as the business is profitable and no one rocks the boat. In the Redstone family, it was Shari, initially, who rocked the boat by looking to solidify her position as the heir apparent of the family business. Shot down by Dad, she had no recourse but to retreat. Next came nephew Michael, again shot down both by Uncle Sumner and the court. In our penchant for litigation to solve a family problem, we lose sight of the fact that we will never get what we really want through the courts. As my colleague, Henry Krasnow put it:

> Many people naively think of litigation as a process that determines who is "right" and who is "wrong," who is guilty and who is "innocent," who is lying and who is telling the truth. To put it more simply, many people think that the litigation process dispenses "justice." (*Your lawyer: An Owner's Manual.* p. 59.)

Yet the fantasy persists that *surely someone with reason* will listen to our plight and will undoubtedly discern that the others are at fault, as anyone with a half a brain can see. But the courts do not seem to work that way many times. We are often left with the dynamics that are played out in different venues, over years and at great cost.

The family playground

Family businesses are different from other businesses. One of the more compelling and problematic issues is that people are related to each other. It really does make a difference that my brother is in the next office or that Dad is down the hall. We all know each other pretty well—and that includes knowing that Tommy didn't change his socks every day in high school to knowing that Mom and Dad did not always get along and that, in fact, they separated for some time a few years ago. These things stay with us, whether we like it or not. Certainly, the memories that we carry around can be a source of good times at Thanksgiving or birthdays, but may not be that much fun when we are negotiating with our brother, father, mother, or sister.

It is always difficult to separate the roles we have in the business from the relationships we have had for many years. It never goes away. It is the nature of the beast.

The dynamic family business

Every family business struggles with the realities of being both a family and a business. The illustration below captures some of this dynamic by dividing the areas of movement and change into the four quadrants. Usually, there is one quadrant (or more) that predominates at a particular time in the life of family and the business. In the Redstone family, for example, the conflict quadrant demanded so much time, energy, and money that little remained for noticing the other three quadrants.

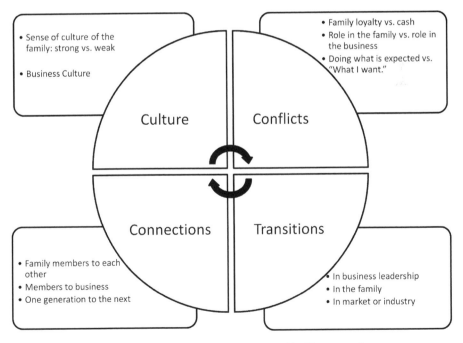

Figure 5-1: The Dynamic Family Enterprise

- **Connections**

Beside the blood ties of each family member to the other, there are the emotional ties. The emotional ties are the "glue" of the family as a unit, and, as such, that glue pulls the members to each other. In the history of every family, there are inevitable conflicts and strains, but one would hope that the family as a unit could find ways to weather the storms and maintain the connections to each member.

Some of these possible connections are:

- Family members to each other
- Members to business
- Later generations to earlier generations

The combinations of all these possibilities are staggering. The one variable over which family members have control, however, is their own understanding and willingness to examine whatever role there are in right now. This means that a family member must be willing to find a way to set aside petty differences and work to resolve substantial issues with another family member. This work is for the good of the business *and* for the good of the family. Establishing clarity of roles and having conversations with other family members about doing so is critical if the entire family enterprise is to grow and develop. This is where many families fall into the inevitable trap of not knowing whom they are supposed to be right now: "Am I family member or business leader?"

- **Conflicts**

Conflicts are part of the territory of just being human and living in a group with other people. How well or poorly the family members negotiate their conflicts will affect how they negotiate the conflicts in the business. If family members have found ways to try to understand each other, to negotiate and find common ground, they will have achieved a milestone that will serve them well on the business side.

The following situations strain any family facing them. In families with poor conflict-resolution strategies, the strains magnify, sometimes to the point that they make very poor decisions.

o Family loyalty versus cash.

o Role in family versus role in business.

o Doing what is expected versus "What I want."

● **Culture**

Each family has its own particular culture that they developed over the years. The Morelli family in chapter 3 not only cared about each other, but also respected each other as individuals.

As the children grew and the company grew, the family's culture, norms, and values became the bedrock of the business. The level of commitment to each other and the willingness to work things out allowed them to find creative ways to grow the company even during a poor economy.

There are two areas to attend to:

o Sense of culture of family: strong versus weak. A strong family culture will have much more positive impact on the emotional tone and structure of the business than one that is weak.

o Culture of the business: is it in line with the family culture or at odds with it?

> When the family culture and the business culture merge in family businesses, they create both a context in which all decisions are made and the glue that holds the family business together. Family patterns, many of which are invisible, become automatic responses to "how we do things around here." The rules, roles, structure, and triangles that each family adopts are expressions of family culture. (Hollander and Bukowitz, p. 141)

● **Transitions**

Periods of transition test the durability and depth of the family's connection to each other, their ability to negotiate conflicts, and their culture as a family. Transitions can either be smooth, planned, and worked through or stormy, unplanned, and unending. The latter situation can have dire financial consequences for the family members, as well as poor outcomes for the business itself. These are the circumstances in which, because of the lack of planning and coordination, the business must be sold, leaving family members with little to show for the many years of hard work. Unfortunately, this occurs all too often, particularly when the family assumes that they can sell the business any time they want, making them all quite wealthy.

These transitions below may be smooth or blow up into crises. Some transitions are:

- o In the business leadership: the need to move to a professional leadership in the company can cause tremendous strain if blood trumps good business sense.

- o In the family: decline in the health of family members, death, or other losses due to alcohol or drug addiction.

- o In the market or industry: demand for the product weakens as cheaper versions are introduced.

Over the life of the family enterprise, one quadrant may "balloon" and demand more attention than at other times. It is a dynamic system and thus, keeps changing. Periods of transition see one quadrant increasing or decreasing in importance. The Barbosas, who we will discuss now, are transitioning their business to new leadership. They are a good example of a family in which there is a lot of energy in the *transitions* quadrant. When conflicts and threats to family connections are out of control, the results can be catastrophic to both family and business. The Redstone family is illustrative of this major breakdown in both areas.

An enterprising family

When Alice and Frank Barbosa started thinking seriously about starting their own business, they were very excited and terrified at the same time. They had always wanted to work for themselves and not have to answer to anyone else. They also knew the tremendous risk of starting a business as Frank had seen when his own father began his business, which eventually failed. He did not want to make the same mistakes. Alice had witnessed her uncle Tony and her father attempt to expand their restaurant into a larger, more upscale space, only to see it all turn to dust. Frank and Alice knew all too well that small businesses, especially restaurants, open and close all the time—sometimes quicker that you can flick a light switch.

So, in 1954 when they opened the first *Alice's Great Dish*, a restaurant featuring Alice's recipes, they knew the risks, and they jumped at the opportunity to do it their own way. In the early years, with two children to care for, they traded shifts and worked long hours seven days a week. With the help of the in-laws and uncles and cousins, they made it work. In the ensuing years, the restaurants became *Just Alice* with the addition of *Just Alice Two*, with three and four coming down the line.

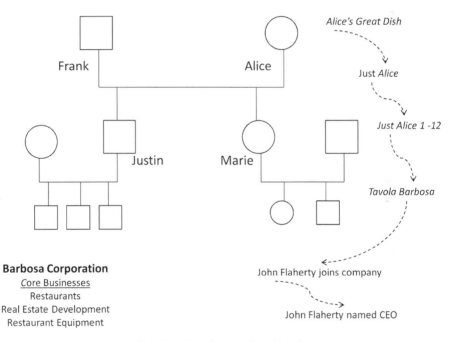

Figure 5-2: The Barbosa Family Genogram

They enjoyed their life as the owners and operators of a successful group of restaurants, and their children, Justin and Marie, spent a lot of time at the restaurant. At first the children mostly hung around, but eventually they began bussing tables and waiting on patrons. As the popularity of the restaurants grew, Alice and Frank freed up enough cash and reinvested in the business. They not only bought new equipment but also began acquiring the properties themselves, so that by the mid-1970s they had twelve *Alice's* restaurants spread throughout the Los Angeles area. They also expanded into suburban locations, as the suburbs were just beginning to boom.

The *Barbosa Corporation*, as it was now known, had many real estate holdings. Alice and Frank worked very much as a team and made joint decisions about almost everything. As the number of locations grew, this became increasingly difficult; many times they would only see each other at home late at night.

They also seemed to make good strategic moves, taking over competitors' locations or moving into the area and making it impossible for the competitor to survive. At the end of the 70s they hired John Flaherty to manage most of the business and oversee day-to-day operations. Justin and Marie were in their twenties and were not working in the business. Justin, a marketing major at a university, had enjoyed all aspects of the business, but upon graduation felt that he just needed to get some space for a while and moved to Florida. He took a job in a real estate company that was expanding in response to a major building boom. He worked on the marketing side of the business and enjoyed not only that aspect of the business but the growth and development of the business itself. Marie married upon graduation from college and took a position in a restaurant equipment manufacturing and distribution company not far from their hometown.

Although Alice and Frank would have enjoyed having the kids in the business, they understood the need for them to spread their wings, get new experiences, and test themselves in other areas of their lives. When Justin married, he began talking about wanting to return home and maybe get involved in the business. He had been in Florida for five years and had learned a tremendous amount about real estate development and marketing.

By 1980, there were twenty-five restaurants in southern California. Some retained the *Alice's* name, but most were now called *Tavola Barbosa*. They catered to patrons who appreciated wholesome Italian food and fresh ingredients. With catering and the three banquet facilities in the region, the Barbosa name became synonymous with "Great food at a reasonable price," as they said in their TV ads. Prominently displayed at the entrance to each restaurant was the sign *Welcome to Our Table.*

Welcome to
Our Table

Justin, now thirty-one and Marie, twenty-nine, both were in the business full time. Justin spent some of his time scouting locations for new restaurants and the rest of his time looking at real-estate development deals throughout the region. They opened a suburban housing development outside San Diego in 1985. It sold out in fourteen months, despite the real estate slump. Marie spent most of her time in the restaurant equipment division. The division now included new equipment sales and repair, and restaurant interior design.

In 1992, John Flaherty was named CEO of the *Barbosa Corporation,* as it was clear that he was invaluable to the growth of the company and was almost like family. The subject of succession came up often in the meetings John had with Alice and Frank. They were now in their mid-sixties and thinking about spending less time in the business and more time with each other and the grandchildren. They had homes in California and Colorado, and wanted to spend more time traveling and visiting friends.

As a family, including John Flaherty, they joined the local university family business center. They found the programs very helpful and the relationships with other family business members a great way to hear about what other families were thinking about and doing, particularly about succession.

Later that year, John, Alice, and Frank announced to the shareholder's meeting that John would retire in five years. They needed a plan for a smooth transition to the new leadership. At this juncture Justin was running operations for real estate, while Marie ran the restaurant division. At this meeting, Alice and Frank also announced that the transition to new leadership would be an open process. Alice said, "We love our kids very much, and you are doing a great job for the company. But Dad and I feel that we need to look at the needs of the business first and put our family relationships second to that. This will be hard for all of us." With that, they outlined a plan that they had constructed with their family business adviser, Tony Rodriguez, himself from a family restaurant business. In this plan, they began a process allowing Justin and Marie to apply for the top leadership positions in the company. They also opened the search to nonfamily candidates.

Justin and Marie were astounded by this turn of events and both felt hurt. With time, however, they had some good, constructive conversations with Mom and Dad and came to understand that this all could be a good process, however it turned out. They were nervous about the competitive aspect, but they understood that this was about trying to make some good decisions in the best interest of the business. They could live with it.

The shareholders voted to stay with Tony Rodriguez as their adviser and consultant during this process. Tony's job was to outline a process for the next five years in which both Justin and Marie would be evaluated for leadership positions, if they were interested, and other applicants would be evaluated as well.

Based on the job descriptions and the discussions within the family and with the board, the transition process unfolded without a lot of fanfare or problems. With agreements about strategy and the need for professional leadership, the process became one part of the overall strategy. The most important and the most difficult piece occurred in the first year when getting agreements, buy-in from all parties, and working through disagreements was expected and normal. The commitment from all stakeholders to the process contributed to its success.

The figure below represents the job description for CEO of Barbosa Corp. This document was used for the search. A similar document for COO was also generated, with a focus on operational experience, training, and education.

CHIEF EXECUTIVE, **BARBOSA CORP.**

Summary

- Provide leadership to position the company at the forefront of the industry.

- Develop a strategic plan to advance the company's mission and objectives, and to promote revenue, profitability, and growth as an organization.

- Oversee company operations, in collaboration with the COO, to ensure efficiency, quality, service, and cost-effective management of resources.

Major Functions/Accountabilities

- Implement the strategic goals and objectives of the organization.

- Create and build the human organization that is aligned with the strategy of the company.

- With the chair, enable the board to fulfill its governance function.

- Give direction and leadership toward the achievement of the organization's philosophy, mission, strategy, and its annual goals and objectives

Reports to   Board of Directors

Responsibilities

- Supports operations and administration of board by advising and informing board members, interfacing between board and staff, and supporting board's evaluation of chief executive.

- Oversee functions of COO.

- Oversees design, marketing, promotion, delivery, and quality of programs, products, and services.

Experience

- Experience in strategic planning and execution in businesses similar to the core business of the *Barbosa Corp.* These include restaurant operations, restaurant development, and real estate.

- Knowledge of contracting, negotiating, and change management. Skill in examining and reengineering operations and procedures.

- Experience in formulating policy, and developing and implementing new strategies and procedures.

- Ability to develop financial plans and manage resources.

- Ability to analyze and interpret financial data.

Transition plan

In line with the goal that John would be retiring within five years, Tony set about crafting a plan for choosing a successor. This transition plan had several components. He created the plan through many discussions with each family member and with John. The process, including the time line, looked like this:

Year One	Develop job description. Tony worked with the family and John to develop the job descriptions for both CEO and COO. The purpose was to ensure that all involved, including the board, would be clear about the requirements of the position, what the qualifications in terms of education and experience would be, and what the ideal candidates would look like in terms of personality. It took the better part of the first year to reach agreement on all of these points.
Year Two	Begin the selection process. With Tony's guidance, candidates were approached and the initial screening process began. With the family's many connections in the business, several good candidates emerged. Justin and Marie threw their hats into the ring at this point. They excused themselves from the discussions about candidates. A committee of the board, consisting of John and two other board members participated in the selection process.
Year Three	With several candidates identified for each position, interviews began. The committee of the board conducted the interviews as a group. At the end of the year the final three candidates for each position were presented to board for consideration. Justin and Marie were in these groups.
Year Four	The board voted unanimously for each candidate, and they were chosen.
Year Five	Justin assumed the position of CEO, and Marie became COO of *Barbosa Corp.*

Figure 5-3: The Transition Process

Transparency

The issue of transparency is significant in a process such as choosing the next leadership for the family enterprise. In the case of the Barbosas, there were no side deals made or promises about one or other of the children becoming leaders of the business. With the help of advisers, they were able to maintain that transparency. The decisions about who would lead the company were as objective as they could possibly be. The major issue was that the business needed professional leadership, such as they have had with John Flaherty. Without that commitment to the process, the transition would not have been as smooth as it had been.

In the course of the process, over a five-year period, Justin and Marie had not only proved themselves worthy of being leaders of the company, but they sought out experiences and education that would help them develop necessary skills and fill in the gaps in their experience. For example, Marie did have a good head for numbers, but she had little in the way of any education in finance. She had learned on the job and knew enough to do her job at present. However, to step into a higher-level position she needed to learn more.

She set out a plan to spend more time with the accountants, while she completed an executive-MBA program at a university business school. It not only gave her "more tools for her toolbox" but also gave her much more confidence and knowledge about the financial end of the business.

She also sought out stretch assignments with the help of John. She was very comfortable in the restaurant equipment end of the business but had not developed herself in the area of marketing and sales. He suggested that she immerse herself in some of the functions in marketing. Within that group, she worked with the internal group, as well as with the consultants they hired.

Like his sister, Justin sought out stretch assignments and identified the areas he needed to develop if he were to become a top leader in the company. John Flaherty and Tony Rodriguez spent considerable time and energy with both Justin and Marie to identify where they needed to learn more from mentors and coaches, where they needed more experience, and in what areas they needed more education. Over four years they each focused not only on the day-to-day aspects of their current positions, but they also devoted considerable time and energy to their growth plans. By the time they were actually applying for and being considered for the positions they desired, they had more experience and education to show for themselves, than if they had just been appointed to these positions. This was not a case of being "groomed" for these positions, as much as developing themselves into legitimate contenders in the race to the top.

Clarification of roles: John, Justin, and Marie

Through the process of transition, both Justin and Marie clarified not only their current roles, which enabled them to be better managers and leaders, but also their thinking about how their roles fit with the overall strategic direction of *Barbosa Corp.* They began thinking more like business leaders and less like family members. They focused on the business and brought their critical-thinking skills to bear on the real-time business problems that they faced. Any sense of entitlement vanished as they moved through the process.

⌘   ⌘   ⌘

Checklist

✓ Separate your own wishes from those of your loved ones.

✓ Separate roles in the business from family relationships.

✓ Don't blame.

✓ Talk to each other.

✓ Plan, plan, plan transitions.

✓ Have a strategy and execute it for the growth of the business *and* the family.

✓ Be transparent.

✓ Create job descriptions

Six

Money, Monet, and Mom

Nobody wanted Mom

As Martha Bluestone approached her eighty-fifth birthday, she hoped that at least one of her children would remember to send a card. Things had not gone well the last few years. After the death of her husband, Roderick, five years ago, the children had become more distant, visited infrequently, and rarely called. She could not recall the last time she had seen any of her seven grandchildren. It must have been a few Christmases ago. It seemed like quite a long time.

But things had been going downhill for many years. Duncan, the oldest, was still very angry over the changes she had made to her estate plan. When Rod died, she reconsidered her initial wish to leave everything to the kids. After all, the family had been prominent in Boston and Palm Beach for several generations, and they needed to give back in some way for all their good fortune. That fortune had been immense at one time and speculation about its current size had sparked some heated debate among the children. Rod and Martha had played it close to the vest, divulging little about the family's actual worth. The girls, Candace and Page, had appeared understanding of their parents' position, but they had married well and were secure. As Duncan observed, "I guess if I had to work, I would. But really, there is so much to do besides going to an office every day. Dad did that, and he didn't seem very happy." Indeed Dad was not happy, although he did work at the law firm founded by his grandfather. He was a named partner but did little to promote either himself or the firm. He was content with what he did there, although other members of the firm viewed him as mostly the name on the door.

Duncan and his father had never been close, although they shared similar interests, such as fly-fishing and polo. Indeed, no one in the family seemed close to any other member. Mom had her interests, especially the flower show and children's charities, which had occupied much of her time until recently. Candace, while an outstanding student at Mt. Holyoke, never developed a passion for academics or anything else, for that matter. Page, the youngest, developed some bad habits in boarding school. She smoked marijuana and drank "a bit too much sometimes," as she said.

During the ensuing year after her husband's death, Martha undertook several significant changes to her estate plan. With her trusted attorney and long-time friend, Clark Appleby, she established a family office to manage the array of assets for the family. The children had been opposed to this, as they felt that things were fine the way they were, and the structure of the several trusts had been in place for many years. Martha had other plans. It was not that she did not care for her children or wish them well in their lives, but she realized that they had lived a life of indulgence and privilege. They were living as if they were entitled to the family wealth. The children weren't particularly motivated to work or be productive in some way because they saw no need for it. As they had been comfortable with the income from their trusts, they arranged their lives based on the assumption that Mom and Dad would always provide.

The year that Duncan decided that it might be fun to start a company spotlights some of the ongoing family dynamics and the unraveling of the titanium threads that bound them. Since college at a "not quite Ivy school," as his mother pointed out many times, he had an interest in the types and varieties of tea from around the world. Shortly before his father's death, Duncan drew up a business plan to develop and market a line of rare organic tea. He envisioned that he would sell his line in all of his favorite stores. He and his friends thought it to be a fabulous idea. Thus, was born the *Fabuloso Tea Company*, with Duncan as its president and CEO. He remembered the stories from his parents about how the Bluestones had acquired their wealth. In particular, he recalled his father going on at some length about his great grandfather, Jethro Bluestone, creating the concept that blossomed into five-and-dime stores. In the late 1870s, *Bluestones* was the big hit in Denver, where the family had settled in the early 1840s. The story of how his great-grandfather hit on the idea of the "little bit of everything store" was compelling.

The story goes that Jethro, although successful as a merchant running a number of general/dry goods stores, thought that he could expand them to include more items that would appeal to the city dwellers in Denver. He always had been an ambitious man and had his sights on building a new, big company. With his entrepreneurial spirit and some cash, he opened the first Bluestone five-and-dime on Market Street in October 1872. The city was growing by leaps and bounds, particularly because of the number of railroad junctions there. The creation of the Denver and Rio Grande Railroad (D&RG) in 1870 opened the route for goods to come more cheaply from Mexico via the railroad. *Bluestone's Everything Store,* as it was called, offered quality, low-cost goods from Mexico, as well as essentials for the home and ranch. It *did* have a little bit of everything.

From that store, as they say, "the rest was history." By 1915, there were seventy-five stores in the western states, all the way from Washington state to New Mexico. It was a huge success, making the family enormously wealthy. They were not the Rockefellers, but they "did well enough," as great grandpa would observe.

With many stories of the successes of the family in business, it was no wonder that Duncan thought he could become a part of that lore. In the present, there was no longer an operating business. There was only an intricate web of holdings representing the hard work of the Bluestone family over many generations.

Duncan had never worked at any job for very long (or very hard for that matter). He thought he had a great idea. When he approached Dad for seed money for *Fabuloso Tea,* Dad stared at the business plan. "This isn't a business plan. It is a fantasy. What, did you cook this up with your polo friends?" Dad scoffed at the idea that Duncan could succeed at anything more than attend the major social events of the season. Turned down by Dad, Duncan approached Mom, who always had a "soft spot in her heart" (as she said) for Duncan, although the two were not close. They seemed to believe that they must be close because he was the first and only son. In fact, they were distant but cordial.

Mom funded the *Fabuloso Tea Company*. In fact, within two years she had shelled out nearly four million dollars for R&D, leasing property, and undertaking contracts with suppliers and manufacturers. Since Duncan did not have expertise in any area of tea growing, processing, manufacturing, marketing, or distribution, he relied heavily on the advice and counsel of others, many of whom lacked real-world business experience. The idea of his tea selling in high-end stores across the country was most appealing. Unfortunately, the design and execution of a solid business plan was beyond his abilities, although he had an MBA from a "pretty good school," as Mom referred to it.

Duncan was devastated when all his efforts resulted in the company filing Chapter 11. Neither Mom nor Dad would bail him out. His dad saw this as yet another example of Duncan "not being cut from the same cloth" as the revered, ancestral Bluestones. Duncan, usually quite upbeat, with a positive attitude and winning smile, sunk into a deep depression. Duncan had been plagued by bouts of depression on and off for many years, but this depression was his worst. He spent three months in the best psychiatric facility on the East Coast and gradually revived. Upon his release from the hospital, he was lost, directionless, and uninterested even in his long list of social activities. During this time, his sisters rarely visited. Dad was diagnosed with stomach cancer and was losing ground rapidly. In the midst of this maelstrom stood Mom, ever stoic, firm lipped, and ramrod straight. The family was coming apart. Her drinking, always a problem but never discussed, worsened, contributing to her blurred vision of what was happening before her eyes.

When Dad died, the girls, Duncan, and Mom retreated from each other. It was during this time that Mom revised her entire estate plan. She changed her will so that the grandchildren would be provided for with various trusts, but each of her own children would receive comparatively little from the vast fortune. When Candace and Page caught wind of the changes, they arrived one afternoon to have a chat with Mom. Although cordial, Mom was neither particularly warm nor welcoming. The three sat rather stiffly in a large room in the mansion. With the girls on the couch and Mom seated almost fifteen feet away and sipping a very dry martini, the distance was palpable and real. Only the art on the walls bore witness to the chill in the air. Martha would not discuss any of the changes to the estate. She hinted that she was considering some changes but offered no details. She wished them well and sent them on their way.

With her eighty-fifth birthday a few days away, Martha received a few proper notes from long-time friends and acquaintances. None offered to meet for tea or a drink. Her own siblings were long gone, as were Rod's.

On the night of her birthday, her personal assistant discovered her sprawled on the plush carpet in the master suite. She died of a massive heart attack in the ambulance on the way to the hospital.

The week after the funeral, the children gathered with Clark Appleby to review the will. Just as they feared, they each received little from the $200 million estate. The grandchildren were well provided for with irrevocable trusts. The bulk of the estate was divided between a family foundation administered by someone of Clark Appleby's choosing and various charities. The houses in Newport, Palm Beach, and Boston were to be sold, and the proceeds given to the Denver Symphony and the Boston Council for the Arts. What remained was a substantial collection of various pieces of art, mostly paintings. These were held in the basement vault of the Beacon Hill Trust Company. In the terms of the will, each child, from the oldest to the youngest, would choose a painting. Any remaining paintings not chosen by the children were to be donated to charity or be thrown in the trash. After each had chosen his or her painting, they turned, nodded, and exited the vault. The bank trust officer closed and locked the massive vault door on the one painting leaning against the back wall, the portrait of their mother, Martha.

Healthy families?

We learn about life and how to live it when we live in a family. Candace, Page, and Duncan, for example, learned well from their parents. They learned about putting up a front and looking good for others. They failed to learn how to manage their lives, how to live according to one's values, or what it means to be real and genuine as a person. The tragedy of their family resides not so much in the last act, but in the very fabric of the family itself: the legacy passed down from one generation to the next. Somewhere along the line, there was a shift away from valuing hard work and commitment. Gradually, the family had lost its emotional center, as had each member. The Bluestone family became unhealthy.

In chapter 2, we discussed the concept of healthy business families and unhealthy business families. The healthy families are those that are industrious regarding the business and united as a family. They create value for both the family and the business. The least healthy business families are those that consume value and are highly conflicted. When considering the overall picture of healthy families, much of this model applies. Looking at the issue of conflict, however, it is clear that some families are not conflicted (at least to the outside observer) because they are deeply disengaged from each other. They have withdrawn from the conflict, and at least on the surface, they appear to get along okay. Rod Bluestone, for example, could have found a way to be supportive of his son's efforts to "make something of himself," without demolishing him emotionally. He could have been the hard-nosed businessman and asked the tough questions about the business plan. He could have found a way to offer guidance to his son, instead of deriding and dismissing him. It was a missed opportunity to offer real help, instead of an opportunity to make him feel stupid, inept, and worthless.

In painting the picture of the ideal family, it would *not* be one without conflict. Rather, it would be a family whose members truly care for one another, are committed to the values and goals of the family, and will work with each other to get

> How bad is bad and how good is good when it comes to families?

through the difficult times and issues. Conflict is inevitable. It is one element of the ongoing tension that exists in any group of people, who are trying to both meet their own needs and still be committed to the good of the group.

How bad is bad and how good is good when it comes to families? Can a family get along well enough and be harmonious to some degree, so that they are productive as a family and have some sense of order? These are not great hurdles; we don't expect anyone to be icons of perfect family happiness. But they should be reasonably balanced in their family life, so that members of the family are productive (the children attend school and are successful in their pursuits, for example).

We all know poorly functioning families. We make our judgments based on, perhaps, our own experience with them, or on the information we have gained from other sources about them. These are the families, for example, for whom any issue, large or small, has the potential to cause a tsunami to sweep through the neighborhood. Alternatively, they are the families who just seem "too good to be true," perhaps because they superficially present well but are emotionally disengaged from each other.

We bring our childhood with us into adulthood. Our own judgments about families are inextricably bound up with our own experience. If you grow up with an alcoholic parent, for example, your perceptions and expectations are deeply and forever colored and shaped by that experience. We may be more distrusting of others' intentions or be ready for violence to erupt or blunt our emotions when faced with conflict. We may work hard not to react based on our life histories, but that takes discipline, self-knowledge, and a willingness to change.

Perhaps, then, it is not so much about a "healthy" family as much as a family that is "good enough" in the way it deals with conflicts and emotions, with each family member demonstrating a willingness to work together for the good of the family. Much like a sports team, the members will work together for the good of the team because they all want to succeed and feel good about themselves. Like sports teams, some families are just outstanding in all ways and others are just okay.

The Bluestones and emotional distance

One of the more insidious and potentially intractable issues in some families is the lack of emotional connectedness. With these families, the emotional distance is cavernous. The children in such circumstances, if they are fortunate, have the benefit of a loving and warm nanny or other caretaker. Such relationships become exceedingly important to these children, as, otherwise, they are bereft of real connection to the family and their siblings. The siblings themselves may provide that connection for each other. In the Bluestone family, that connectedness was missing. The children sometimes did talk about Concetta, one of the full-time nannies who lived with the family for many years. When Mom dismissed her when Duncan was fourteen, the children were devastated and were furious with their mother. Mom had some ostensible reason for the dismissal, but the children suspected that the real reason was that Concetta had such a warm relationship with each of them that their mother was jealous. Of course, there was never any forum to address that part of the equation with her. Father showed no interest in the matter whatsoever.

> A legacy of empty houses, empty emotions, and empty relationships.

Although the children did have some good years with a caring person, the loss of Concetta was, for Duncan and his sisters, a profound one. Over time that sadness and grief hardened into a shell of selfishness and emotional isolation. Perhaps this is the heritage in this family: a legacy of empty houses, empty emotions, and empty relationships.

The family

A family is a grouping of individuals who are related to each other. The basics remain essentially the same: this is a group that lives in the same dwelling and shares meals together, with each member contributing to the life of the family unit. The typical American family no longer exists as it did some fifty years ago. There can be great instability, as members leave and the family reconfigures itself. Individuals dissolve previous marriages, marry, and bring their own children into the new family unit—a blended family. The face of the family has changed.

The issues of stability, family boundaries, conflict, and change are all pieces of the puzzle of families that are in business together. As we have seen, these families bring their own family *stuff* to all of their endeavors, for good or ill.

The family system

The family is primarily an *emotional* system: members of the family have emotional relationships with each other and are bound to each other because of these emotional ties. As an emotionally charged system, it does not always act rationally. As a system, there are (or should be) built-in mechanisms for self-correction. When, for example, Duncan Bluestone approached his father with his ideas for his tea company, his father was dismissive and belittling. He did not encourage or assist his son. Quite the contrary, he made it clear that Duncan could not measure up to the ancestors who created the family wealth. Of course, if father had only looked at himself in the mirror, he would have noticed that he was but a pale reflection of those same entrepreneurial forebears. Duncan ran to Mom, mostly for the money, as he received no solace from her. The family just did not seem to find a way to meet each other emotionally.

The family consists of individuals, yet it acts like a system. Conflicts are inevitable because each person has unique needs and desires that may be at odds with the goals or needs of the group. There are smaller groupings within the larger group, such as two-person groups called *dyads* or three-person groups called *triads*. With the movement of the couple away from being a dyad and becoming a family (triad) with arrival of a baby, the entire group changes. Couples go through all the adjustments of making room for baby and accepting this new little person into their lives. They feel the stress of that expanded relationship. As a dyad, the couple has the opportunity to work out their conflicts over time, with each individual negotiating and compromising along the way for the good of their relationship. The name of the game as a couple is negotiation and compromise.

In attempting to resolve conflict or maintain stability in the two-person system, sometimes the couple involves a third person. This person, the other leg of a triangle, serves to create an alliance and restore harmony to the relationship. This person sometimes is the wife's girlfriend, who is willing to hear the wife's troubles. Alternatively, it is the old friend of the husband. Many times the addition of the third person helps the couple get back to a sense of equilibrium.

With the addition of children to the mix of the original dyad, the web of relationships extends and becomes increasing more complex. Many families do just fine because they have worked out how they will maintain all the relationships and still maintain the balance in the family. In some business families, there is never peace. This happens precisely because, in their history as a family, they have never adjusted and compromised so that they can maintain some tranquility. These families are in a constant state of conflict, turmoil, and bad feeling. What one observes in their present-day relationships is a reflection and mix of many past, unresolved conflicts. The present, in these families, does repeat the past.

In considering the Bluestones in this regard, we have little to go on about Martha and Roderick's early relationship. Given what we have seen about the children and Mom in her later years, we might speculate a bit:

- It is very likely that Mom and Dad, although "compatible" in social circle terms, may not have been mature enough or developed enough personality wise to be good parents

- Judging from the interaction of Duncan and his father, such cold nastiness belies an inconsiderate, selfish, and narcissistic man who is unable to wish his son well

- The children seemed more interested in the art than in Mom—a sad statement of their own inability to be generous or empathic adults

- This was a family of self-involved and self-focused individuals. This is in contrast to the Morellis and Barbosas discussed previously. Those families deeply cared about each other and worked together to create a wonderful business together; the Bluestones cared little for each other in any genuine way, did little for the greater good of humanity, and seemed rather empty and pathetic in their clawing and scratching to get what they believed they deserved.

Common family dynamics

- ### Triangulation

As we mentioned briefly above, triangles occur in every system of more than two people.

A triangle is a three-person relationship system. It is the building block of larger emotional systems because a triangle is the smallest stable relationship system. A two-person system is unstable because it tolerates little tension before involving a third person. A triangle can contain much more tension without involving another person because the tension can shift around three relationships. If the tension is too high for one triangle to contain, it spreads to a series of "interlocking" triangles.

In the Bluestone family, for example, when Father rejected Duncan in his efforts to get his tea company off the ground, Duncan went to his mother. Mother provided the relief valve that Duncan needed—she also provided the cash for *Fabuloso Tea!* In terms of family dynamics, this move allowed the family to maintain some stability in the face of a potentially explosive situation. Had Duncan and Roderick actually been able to discuss their differences, maybe "duke it out" and reach some agreement about going forward or not, it might have been a real breakthrough for the family. But this did not occur. Duncan and Father played the roles they had each carved out over time. The family dynamic was one in which no member ever truly dealt with the emotions of any other member to either resolve conflict or stabilize their relationship. This type of dynamic runs rampant in family enterprises. If there is no counteracting force to correct it, it becomes a deep, unspoken and intractable "way of doing things" in the family.

You might wish that Candace or Page had intervened to support Duncan and get Father to deal with him. This did not happen. In this family, the triangles served not to resolve issues but to mask them and drive them underground.

● Splitting

Triangulation can also result in *splitting,* in which one person plays the third family member against another. Preadolescent girls typify this dynamic, usually when one girl in the triad is made the object of scorn or ridicule, while the other two (sometimes former friends) bad-mouth her behind her back. Sometimes this results in *scapegoating* of one family member. This person is blamed for the family problems or the current state of affairs: "If Jennifer would get her act together and stop giving us such a hard time about the buy/sell agreement, we would just get it done. She is always doing that." An extreme and very destructive example of this scapegoating is *character assassination*, which is a systematic attempt to destroy the reputation of the other person.

● Insiders and outsiders

Martha Bluestone must have sensed, perhaps unconsciously, that she was the outsider in the relationship of the children with Concetta, the nanny. Since Mother retained the power in the situation, she could toss out Concetta, perhaps in the hope that somehow the children would be drawn to her. Of course, the opposite occurred, and the children hated her for taking away a good person who loved them. The children distanced themselves from Mother, and she was even more of an outsider to them. They rebuffed her, and she was left alone. Her drinking probably soothed some of her devastating feelings at least temporarily. In a way, the children now formed their own group, as both Mother *and* Father were outside their group. The family never recovered from this, which is another reason why they left Mother's portrait in the vault.

- **Denial**

As they say, "Denial is not just river in Egypt." Denial is one of the most psychologically primitive and destructive mechanisms we use. In its most elementary form, we hear from a child who just shattered a glass on the floor, "I didn't do it. The dog did that." As a protective mechanism, it can be useful to preserve some dignity or self-esteem in a situation in which one is responsible. Criminals, sociopaths, and Ponzi schemers are masters of denial, as any defense lawyer, law enforcement officer, or victim can attest.

> Denial plays a huge part in families coming apart.

Denial was rampant in the Bluestone family. Duncan, for example, when rejected by Father, turned to Mother. He denied within himself his own rage at his father for, once again, rejecting him and treating him like dirt. Mother, instead of using the opportunity to help Duncan deal with his father, accepted the situation, telling herself, "Well, that's just the way he is." Thus she denied her own long-held anger at her husband for being so emotionally unavailable. The complicity and collusion of the entire family in this dynamic has a long and deep history. Whatever the source, perhaps long ago in previous generations, they were unable to deal with each other in any other way than to deny and push aside their own real feelings. They kept up appearances. This pattern became the family's way of operating. The pattern was internalized and became part of the personality of each individual. All of this unresolved emotion, denial, and lack of real connectedness contributed to Mother being left in the vault. The kids denied her importance and existence, leaving her in the dark.

- **Boundary problems**

This term usually refers to how family members draw the line around themselves as a unit, separate from the rest of the world. The Barbosa family ("Welcome to our table") exemplifies a family that had no problems in this area. They did not draw a rigid boundary around themselves. On the contrary, they welcomed others into their family. They trusted each other and cared about each other, which strengthened them and allowed them to appoint John Flaherty as nonfamily CEO of *Barbosa Corp.* The parents encouraged the children to explore other avenues in their lives and did not coerce them into joining the family business. Eventually, each of the children wanted to be a part of the business. They freely made their decisions. And, although Justin and Marie were hurt by Mom and Dad's choice to appoint John CEO, they respected it and eventually could see its wisdom. The family could deal with hurt feelings and still be emotionally honest with each other. This made each of them stronger, and their family more cohesive.

The Bluestones had a weak boundary around them. They were not a cohesive family unit. They could not withstand conflict or strong emotions. The result was that emotions were dampened and suppressed, leaving each person less able to be emotionally competent.

Families with weak boundaries, such as the Bluestones, cannot tolerate emotional discord and flee from it. Other families, with too rigid boundaries, make decisions, for example in the business, based only on family ties, which is a huge mistake. This leads to the position that, "Uncle Sal should be next CEO because it is his turn." Or it leads to distrust of "outsiders." In maintaining such a position, the family loses the flexibility and opportunity to work with consultants and advisers who can be of great help to them.

Entitled or not, here they come

Elsewhere we have talked about issues of arrogance, entitlement, and narcissism in family enterprises. These patterns may be part of the fabric of the family. Advisers and consultants know that when they encounter issues of entitlement in the family business, they have major hurdles to overcome. Young Johnny may feel entitled to become general manager, even though he has little experience and has yet to prove himself in either the family business or elsewhere. If allowed to persist, this pattern of entitlement can prove to be very destructive to the business. Employees see that Johnny is promoted only because he has the right last name and not because he actually is competent to do a great job in another position.

Where does this entitlement come from? Children learn to expect things and to be treated in a certain way from countless interactions in the family. They quickly learn either that they must earn what they want or that they do not have to earn it. It is a culture of privilege that children pick up on early. If children learn that the "regular rules" do not apply to them, they will have no incentive to abide by them. If this pattern is learned early on, they will have exactly the same expectations when they are adults. Certainly, there are children of privilege who learn that there is value in hard work, commitment, and doing one's best. They learn that it is good to accomplish, for example, and get good grades in school. They develop a more "normal" self-concept than do children who have few rules to abide by. The children in the latter group have very poor self-esteem and underneath it all, feel incompetent and worthless. They act as if what they do is of no consequence. That is exactly how they feel—*they* are of no consequence. They learn, as the owner of a large family business once told me, "It doesn't really matter what my son does at work. He will still get the same paycheck. I don't care." The net result is a family member who feels like nothing really makes any difference because "I don't really make a difference."

My colleague and friend, Paul Karofsky, describes what he calls, "Entitlement on Steroids" with these examples:

> "Others will take care of it, it's not such a big deal, they're making too much out of it; it will go away by itself; I don't have to bust my hump to fix things; others will manage the business problems—after all, they've always done so. Just give me a job for the rest of my life."

> "No problem with debt, we'll just borrow more, and if this bank won't help us, we'll find another one; we're only in default on one covenant. It's okay if Dad gives the company a loan. After all, if we put it below the line, the bank will consider it equity and even give us two to one for it!"

> It's an attitude of *noblesse oblige* gone awry, of
> reactions that are cavalier and managed with
> a blindly relaxed approach. It's the belief that
> others will take responsibility. Almost a bit of up-
> to-date Alfred E. Newman's, "What, me worry?"
> (*ffi Practitioner*, spring 2010)

Entitlement is always one part of a larger picture related to one's development within a family. In most families, the reality principle holds sway: the needs, impulses, and desires of the child are shaped to conform to the demands of reality, i.e., the world of other people. In some families, the self-centeredness of the child is not sufficiently tempered or molded. These become the "spoiled kids" who never seem to be told "no" in an authoritative way or held to limits. These kids grow up believing that they can have anything they want, that there are no limits, and, most destructive to their self-esteem, that there are no consequences to their actions. Whether right or wrong, good or bad, they are not responsible, and there is always a way out (or someone will bail them out).

Addicted to Bad Things

There is significant controversy about the role of addictions in family businesses. The lack of solid research makes it difficult to get a clear sense of how extensive a problem addiction is within family enterprises. Many advisers and consultants believe that addictions are an enormous problem in these families.

As we saw with the Bluestones, Mother had a serious, long-standing drinking problem. The toll any addiction takes on a family can be enormous. As her addiction worsened, it signaled Martha's increasing disconnection from her children and from life. Although she denied that she had a problem with alcohol, the psychological consequences to her and the children were undeniable. In most families with an alcoholic parent, that parent not only becomes emotionally unavailable to the children but also does not process emotions in a normal way. Through the haze of whatever drug the parent is addicted to, feeling is blunted and the experience of normal affect (feeling) is diminished. Years later, for example, children of alcoholic parents describe a feeling of not making a difference, not being heard, and of being scared of that parent. The parent does not recall it that way. He or she is unable to. The addicted parent does not process experience or the memory of experience in a normal fashion, i.e., the memories are distorted or unavailable—it is all a fog. For the children, the memories are all too vivid and disturbing.

Addiction in any form takes its toll on everyone in the family in different ways. Candace and Page have different memories than Duncan. Duncan, being the oldest, probably felt responsible for protecting his sisters from their mom, who was unpredictable and unreliable. Given that Father also was emotionally unavailable, it fell to Duncan to be responsible and be the grown up in the situation. This is a tremendous responsibility for a child.

Families that struggle with the addiction of any family member are always battling their own issues of what to do, how to help that person, and what is in the best interests of the family as a whole. They seek the help of medical and mental health professionals and often that can be of great value. At times, however, they are still left trying to figure out the best course. They fear that if they don't do anything that person may commit suicide, die in an auto accident, kill someone else, or accidentally overdose. Their own emotions are very mixed. Mixed with all the feelings of concern for that person are the anger, rage, and terrible disappointment with him or her.

Many children in such circumstances feel robbed of their childhood because they're always worrying about Mom or Dad. In the Bluestone family, the children were left to their own devices and struggled with feeling emotionally abandoned while trying to construct something out of their lives. They had neither the tools nor the support of caring, available parents to succeed. But they did the best they could. They made the best out of a very bad situation.

Consider

Many families find themselves somewhere on the spectrum from being healthy/normal families to being desperate/unhealthy families. The most difficult issue, by far, in finding a way out is overcoming the denial that anything is wrong. Many families manage to stay somewhat stable by colluding with each other and not confronting serious issues. They secretly live in fear that something terrible will happen if they attempt to change the status quo. Change may be risky, but living in fear and hopelessness does not seem like such a wonderful alternative.

Consider these questions if you are looking for a way to deal with family issues as we have discussed here:

- What is the price you pay for doing nothing?
- What is the risk to you as a family if you continue with the way we do things?
- Have you given up? Why?
- What is you greatest fear about the family?
- Are you willing to work to change the current situation?

⌘　⌘　⌘

Checklist

✓ Confront the harsh truths.

✓ Consider the legacy of the family enterprise.

✓ Reach out to each other, especially the "outsiders."

✓ Plan how to move the family forward.

✓ Begin somewhere.

✓ Do not do nothing—denial gets you nowhere.

✓ Don't give up hope.

Seven

Family Trees and Wooden Bumpers

The Gladney Family

When the Gladneys moved to Chicago from Port Royal, South Carolina, in June 1903, they had few possessions. No one in the family had ever been more than fifteen miles outside of Port Royal. Ben and Bertie recalled all too well the hurricane and tidal wave of 1893, which was responsible for the loss of thousands of lives in Port Royal and the surrounding vicinity. The economy of the region was in shambles and jobs were nonexistent.

When they left, they had little to take with them other than some clothes and memories. Bertie's great aunt Ida Mae and cousins had moved to Chicago a few years previously, as there were more opportunities for people of color. Bertie and Ben heard from her that, "Things are certainly better up there than in Beaufort County. There are opportunities for people like us who will work hard." In that same letter, she invited them up, adding that they could stay with her "until you got on your feet."

Life in Chicago was better than Port Royal. The Gladneys stayed with Bertie until they could afford an apartment in the triple decker where Ida Mae lived. Ben landed a job at the newly opened *Holsman Automobile Company*. He had always had a knack for mechanical things and had a keen interest in the new engines. While at *Holsman*, he and his coworkers would work on one car until it was completed. This allowed him to handle and install all the parts and systems on the "high wheeler automobile," from the engine and drive train to the steering and metalwork of the bumpers and fenders. Chicago at the time was the hub of automobile invention and fabrication in the United States, and when *Holsman* closed its doors in 1911, Ben scrambled for work. Cousin Al had opened a small body and fender repair shop in the neighborhood, and Ben joined him there. Business boomed, as they became known as the best body and fender men for the Model Ts, which now clogged the avenues.

Ben eventually opened his own shop, *Gladney's Body and Fender*. Through the twenties and into the thirties, the business grew, and he opened more shops in the surrounding areas. These became full-service repair shops. With five shops, he was doing well. Their children joined the business. With all the growth and expansion, Ben and Bertie looked for ways to get the children in a position to eventually take over. Charlie, the oldest, liked the hands-on repair work. He was a good mechanic and did well with customers. Jimmy, also known as "Royal," had a head for numbers and the business end of things. Charlotte, a young mother of three, worked part time doing bookkeeping.

New business

For several years, a small sideline of the business had been the repair and replacement of auto bumpers. They had paid little attention to this aspect of the business, as it seemed more incidental to the main business. Over time, however, they had accumulated a sizable collection of replacement bumpers. Dealers would contact them looking for replacement parts. They soon realized they could grow that business and fabricate their own replacements, as there was always a need for bumpers for all the cars on the road. Jimmy headed up this part of the business.

The little empire of *Gladneys Auto Repair and Fender* and the new *Royal Bumper Exchange* were growing.

Ben retired in 1949, and the boys decided to separate the businesses. It was a friendly separation as they both saw that they had potential for each business. By the end of WW II, the bumper exchange also included custom metal fabrication for the large expensive cars now on the roads all around Chicago.

By the late sixties, Charlie's son, John, took the helm at the *Gladney Auto Repair Group*, and Royal's son, Toby, took over the *Metal Fabrication and Bumper Group*. While the families grew and developed, they had remained linked because of the enduring family story and the

> Be decent, honest, and fair with your customers, and they will stay with you.

values of commitment to family and hard work. By 1985, a new entity was formed, linking the families once again. The *Gladney Auto Group* as it was now known, consisted of the metal fabrication group, the Bumper Exchange, the Auto Repair, and several new car dealerships. Under the new umbrella, the family elected a nonfamily CEO to head the entire organization.

With Ralph Summer, the nonfamily CEO, in place, the entire family remained committed to Ben's enduring vision, which had driven it both as a family and in its business activities for almost a hundred years: Be decent, honest, and fair with your customers, and they will stay with you. This vision is conveyed to customers and staff alike in every part of the organization. It is what drives the family in all its business ventures.

The evolution of the business looked like this:

1911:   Ben founds *Gladneys Body and Fender*

1920s: Grows to five shops.

Charlotte, Charlie, and James "Royal" join the business

Two new entities: *Gladneys Auto Repair and Fender* and the *Royal Bumper Exchange*

1940s: *Royal Bumper Exchange and Metal Fabrication* expands

1960s: John leads *Gladney Auto Repair Group*

Toby leads *Metal Fabrication and Bumper Exchange*

1985:   Consolidation under *Gladney Auto Group*

Ralph Summer named nonfamily CEO.

2010:   Fourth generation joining the business

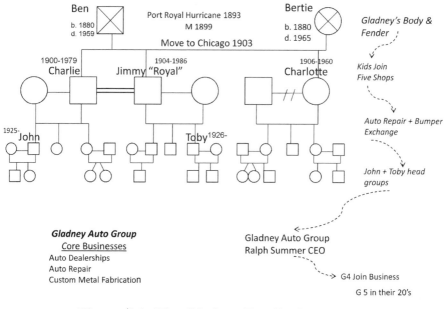

Figure 7-1: The Gladney Family Genogram

How did the Gladneys flourish?

The legacy of Ben and Bertie is remarkable. Like many people seeking better lives for themselves and their children, they sought their fortunes away from home. Although life was tough in Port Royal at the turn of the century, their roots were deep and strong. Their families had endured the worst of the war that divided the states and Reconstruction. Sharecropper's lives were little better than those of the slaves from whom they descended. Indeed, the stories in the Ben and Bertie's families were tales of heartache, disappointment, suffering, and poverty. They were determined to give their children better childhoods than their own and better prospects economically and socially.

Ben and Bertie carried those long-told stories deep in their hearts when, in 1903, they traveled way up to the cold north. They were determined to make a go of it for their little family. They had some family support with Ida Mae and the cousins, but little else. The stories of leaving Port Royal, settling in Chicago, and making a life for themselves were told and retold mostly every Thanksgiving when the extended family gathered for the turkey dinner. Now, over a hundred years after their trek, the great grandchildren listened to stories, some with near-fantastic embellishment. The photos of Ben, Bertie, Charlotte, Royal, and Charlie hung prominently in the homes of the next generations.

They told of how, in the darkest days of World War II, when metal was in very short supply, Ben and the boys worried about the bumper business and the custom metal work that was suffering because of the shortage of metal. They arrived on the idea to craft, as Royal put it, "really fine wooden bumpers." In fact, they began making them, and the bumpers became a big hit around Chicago, as the owners boasted of their "really fine bumpers," a testament to their patriotism, and perhaps their bad driving that got them into the pickle of needing a new bumper in the first place.

Storytelling, remembering and honoring the past, and holding on to the family values of hard work and *stick-to-itiveness* passed from one generation to the next. Scrapbooks filled with photos were proudly passed around the family as a reminder of where they all came from. When the youngest children reached fifth grade family history was a major topic. They marched into class, proud as could be, with the best and biggest painted plywood family tree in the whole school.

This was a proud family, proud of its heritage, the legacy of Ben and Bertie, and proud of its roots in Chicago as a family that cared about its community.

So, why did they flourish as a business? The most important and telling answer, just like the Morellis we have discussed before, emerges from the strength and values of the family itself. As some might say, "It's hard to make a great family business resting on a broken family." We might add, "Great family businesses grow out of great families." Of course, this is a bit simplistic and probably naive, as clearly even among the so-called "great families" there are few that are perfect. It might be more accurate to say that successful family businesses grow from families that manage to

> Successful family businesses grow from families that manage to retain their values, aren't too crazy or out of control, and are pretty good at dealing with conflict and reining in big egos.

retain their values, aren't too crazy or out of control, and are pretty good at dealing with conflict and reining in big egos. That may be a little wordy, but it seems to be in the right direction.

Surely, the Gladneys had their share of problems, big egos, and dysfunctional family members. Overall, they were a good family with the ability to repair itself and keep moving along.

Developing their leaders

As outlined in chapter 1, the leadership development model consists of three parts: people, experiences, and programs. The Gladneys serve as a good example of how this is not a static model but one that changes and adapts over time. For example, with Ben working so hard to build the business for twenty years,

People

Experiences

Programs

there was little consideration of who would succeed or lead the business. He was too busy making sure they would survive. Charlie and Royal not only had an interest in the business, but they also had a close relationship with their father. The three could discuss the needs of the business, argue about how to grow it, and then think through what the next steps might be for them and the business. The boys learned from their father that success was not solely dependent on hard work, although that was important, but that if they were to be successful as a family, they needed to find ways to cooperate, work together, and remain focused on their goals.

In this leadership development scheme, the first step for this family was to maintain and deepen the relationships of the children with Ben and Bertie. As a family team, they made good decisions for themselves and for the business. Charlie and Royal, as second-generation family business members, took on many different roles, thus expanding their own base of understanding of the business. For example, Charlie became an expert at metal fabrication, and when the time came to make a shift to wooden bumpers during WW II, he had little trouble developing the skills he needed to be successful in making "really fine bumpers." And Royal, as he grew to understand more about the finance side of the business, learned how to build and leverage relationships with the bankers who would lend them the capital they needed to grow. These were important skills for each brother to learn, if the business was to flourish into the next generation.

In succeeding generations, formal college education and participation in family business forums became important. John and Toby's children, many of whom worked in various parts of the business, not only had college degrees, but gained a depth of experience in their roles within the company. When they joined the Loyola University family business forum as a group, they benefitted immensely from the formal programs on strategy, human resources, and family dynamics, and they also found the personal connection to the other families encouraging and enlightening.

The leadership development efforts, over time, took on a life of their own, so that by the fourth generation, it was a natural expectation that everyone who would enter the business would learn as much as possible about business and their particular industry. They also bought into one of the many sayings in the family that, "We can all get there a lot faster if we row together than if we argue about who's in charge." With family members mentoring each other or participating in mentoring programs with business colleagues, the culture of the family infused the business. Charlie and Royal often reminded the younger generation of that Ben used to say, "We're all in this together, rowing this boat in the same direction." With that reminder framed on the office wall, the issue of who would assume leadership positions became less important than making sure they were doing what they needed to do to grow the business.

Quarterbacks

The Gladneys were fortunate to have connected with a group of advisers who were willing to come together as a team, as opposed to only working in their individual professional space. This concept, of having an advisory team, although not new, is difficult to achieve. Advisers usually like to do the work they are hired for and leave it at that. It takes more work to create and function as a team, and it usually means that one person needs to serve as the "quarterback" of the team. The need for a quarterback is quite straightforward: in this role, the person can have a bird's-eye view of what each team member contributes to the overall goal of serving the client.

As the business grows, the number of advisers grows with it. At some point, there may be dozens of advisers, including lawyers, CPAs, wealth management professionals, insurance professionals, management and leadership professionals, and family dynamics specialists. Too often, one adviser does not know what the other is doing. The results can be disastrous, or at least inefficient and costly for the client.

For example, when designing an estate plan, the attorney has one set of objectives that will have implications for wealth management and insurance needs. Without good coordination among these professionals, clients may end up with an estate plan that may not serve them well over the long term.

The most simple, cost effective, and efficient solution is that one person serves as the quarterback. In this role, it is the quarterback's responsibility to remain in touch with each adviser, bringing them together as needed to coordinate a strategy, for estate planning, for example. Of course, the client must appreciate the need for and importance of such a move. The integrated team approach, as opposed to the more "siloed" approach can have great benefit for the client.

Governance

- Boards

At some point in the history of the family and the growth of a successful family business, governance structures need to be considered. Very large enterprising families tend to have structures that are more complex. Sometimes it is a matter of the size of the business and the number of family shareholders. Smaller businesses and less complex families may use more informal structures that serve their purposes. For example, many businesses use *advisory boards* to help guide them in their business strategy. Such boards have no power and only serve an advisory capacity. The downside to such boards is that they tend to be populated by family friends, the trusted adviser, or others who may not have sufficient business expertise to be useful to chart the direction of the business. The best boards consist of those with business experience from their own business or have specific skills, such as knowledge of strategy or finance. The best of these boards are balanced according to current needs of the business (not the needs of the owner) and meet regularly to address the business issues facing the company.

The function of the board is to oversee the work of the CEO and the leadership team, and offer advice and counsel regarding the direction of the company. A board with independent (outside) members generally includes experts and experienced business people, each of whom brings a unique contribution to the table. Such a board usually includes some shareholders as a minority.

The board should add value to the business by:

- o Providing guidance to the business leadership and by overseeing finances and operations.

- o Providing strategic direction and identifying growth opportunities.

- o Negotiating and facilitating the tension between the shareholders' needs and the business.

- Team Captains

The Gladneys established an informal system of "team captains." These were family members who, if they worked in one of businesses, took the lead in business in some form. For example, Toby's eldest son, Ben, had a keen interest in the dealerships and worked in them off and on while in college. After graduation, he spent three years working at other dealerships around Chicago, honing his sales skills and learning the business. When he asked his father if he could join the latest of the twelve dealerships, Toby had one question, "Do you think you can make the family proud and yourself happy if you do that?" Young Ben (as he was called) answered, "I know this family, and I know where my name came from. I want to join this business, so that a hundred years from now, people will talk about me the way they talk about great grandpa." Ben joined the business. And with that, Toby set in motion the process for transitioning the business, once again, from one generation to the next.

There were also informal family captains. These were the family members who emerged as leaders in the family. They represented each living generation. They joked that, "You'd better ask Mae about that." Mae, the granddaughter of Charlotte, was a bright young woman with ambitions for herself and the family. She was a lawyer in Chicago, did not work in the business, and was unmarried. She often talked about the legacy of Ben and Bertie and her understanding about her own generation's responsibility to the family and the community. She quietly worked on her plan to establish the *Ben and Bertie Family Foundation*. She was eager to do it and proud that the family was behind her to get it off the ground.

- Family forums

The purpose of *family meetings* or *family councils* is to have a structure that provides for and encourages family participation in decision making, planning, and problem solving related to the business. Their aim is to address the various, and many times competing needs and interests of family shareholders. This is an efficient way to gain input and also consensus on issues critical to the business. Family meetings tend to occur several times during the year because family members are used to having input on the direction of the business in an ongoing way. These meetings are important particularly for family businesses that are in the throes of conflict or experiencing stagnant growth.

Family assemblies are meetings that provide family members an opportunity to learn more about the business, to become educated about the business and the family, and to consider whether they want to join the business.

These family councils and forums have four major functions (See Gersick, 1997):

- To educate family members about the duties of family business ownership

- To clarify the boundary between the family and the business

- To offer a forum for family members to talk about the business that is separate from family social gatherings, and

- To provide a forum for developing a common vision for the family and the business

Over the course of ten years, the Gladneys established and implemented an interconnected web of areas in which family members could participate according to their interests and needs. During that time, they:

o Established a family council

o Wrote a family mission statement called *Taking Care of Business*

o Wrote a family constitution

o Established the *Gladney Family Council*

  - Formed committees for the family forum

  - Wrote an employment policy for family members

  - Wrote a Family Council Handbook

  - Held annual family education forums (the Gladney family assembly)

o Established kinship groups, including sibling groups and a cousin consortium

o Held an annual family retreat for all family members (whether shareholders or not)

o Established the *Ben and Bertie Family Foundation*

o Compiled the 347 recipes for the *Gladney family cookbook*

Taking Care of Business

Our Values

Our family has a long history. Our values are rooted in the lives and work of Ben and Bertie Gladney. They represent all that we hold dear: the importance of hard work, devotion to the family, and always striving to better our community and ourselves.

- We value honesty above all.
- We value creativity, innovation, and "thinking big" in the business.
- We value giving back to the community in a real, meaningful way.
- We value our children as those who will make this a better world than the one we gave them.
- We value independence, toughness, AND humility.

Our Business

Our business is important to us. We work hard and will continue to do so in the business no matter what our role or function. We want the best for our customers and put them first.

Our business grew out of and is an integral part of our "family enterprise." They are linked and experience all the problems that brings!

We will make good decisions for the business and not be swayed or inflamed by pettiness, self-centeredness, or allegiance to one part of the family or another.

We welcome family members into the business. We will establish guidelines for family members joining the business so that they know what is expected of them.

We will establish a board of directors to help us make good business decisions. We will listen to them.

We will do our best to remember which hat we are wearing; we will leave the family hat at home when at work and the work hat at work when at home.

Our Vision

We work hard to refine and cultivate our vision for this family and its business. Our vision is to keep our eye on the prize—a thriving, vibrant business and an energetic, focused family committed to our values and ideals.

Our vision is to create an enterprising Gladney family, with lots of moving parts that all work together.

We want to give back to our community and for this, we have created the *Ben and Bertie Charitable Foundation.* The vision for this foundation is to create and support educational programs for our young people in our community to enable them to pursue their dreams through education.

Our Mission

Our mission is tied to our vision. We strive to deepen and extend the values and ideals of this family both in the business and out. Our mission is to be one family, doing many interesting, cool things, in the business and out, but all activities in line with who we are, where we came from, and where we want to go.

⌘　⌘　⌘

Are the Gladneys a Healthy Family?

Recently researchers have identified four components that help create a climate of trust in a family business.

These are:

- **Character:** integrity, honesty, and credibility; being perceived as a "good person"
- **Competency:** skills, expertise, and performance indicating good judgment and decision making.
- **Predictability:** follow-through, keeping promises, and consistency.
- **Caring:** demonstrating genuine interest in the well-being of others; empathy and understanding. (LaChapelle and Barnes, 1-17.)

The Gladneys seem to be hitting on all four cylinders. They are a family rooted in and driven by their values and history. As seen in their mission statement, they aim to keep that entrepreneurial edge through each generation. They do not shy away from conflict but welcome it. The latest generation represented by John and Toby, see their roles as guardians of the family legacy. Thus, their disagreements are about strategy and execution, and not about personality or ego. They respect each other and deeply understand that they are in the process of building not an empire but a true family enterprise that is in sync with the values of the past and the vision for the future.

This family has all of the major components of a "dynamic family enterprise":

- **Connections**

The Gladneys are connected to all family members and welcome the "newcomers" into the fold. There is room for all, with the expectation that each will contribute to the good of the family. They are connected to the business, either through working in it or by their involvement in the family council.

- **Culture**

They have a very strong sense of family culture and do all they can to foster that connection in the succeeding generations. This sense of culture spills over to the business, so that everyone in the business knows this is a real family business.

- **Transitions**

They pay attention to developing the next generation in the business and in the family. In the business, transitions are planned, and potential leaders are given opportunities to expand their experience and knowledge base about the business. Nonfamily leaders are welcomed into the business, as they offer perspectives, education, and experience sometimes lacking within just the family itself.

- **Conflicts**

Money always complicates things, and the Gladney family is no exception. They have worked out the sticky situations of family who do not work in the business yet are shareholders. They have found ways to reach compromises that everyone can live with, as opposed to everyone getting what they want or think they deserve.

Leaders and Followers

If there are leaders, then there are followers. Even in such a cohesive, down-to-earth family, there are the inevitable conflicts and bruised egos over succession planning in the business—not everyone can be the next CEO or CFO. The plan that the Gladneys put in place, many years ago, still operates. With their employment guidelines for family members and the requisite mix of education, experience, and maturity, the leaders have emerged with little controversy.

With the family culture emphasizing honesty, collaboration, humility, and commitment, the leadership issues have been resolved with no splits or factions in the family. This is quite remarkable, as most families at some point suffer some major fracture, which can often doom the family and the business.

What the Gladneys accomplished

In line with the family business transition checklist (chapter three), this is what the Gladneys accomplished:

<u>For the business</u>

- Created a strategic plan
- Chose a successor
- Designed a contingency plan for succession
- Developed the top leadership

<u>For the owners</u>

- Transferred ownership and control
- Empowered the team of owners
- Crafted a policy for family participation in the business
- Created a board of directors with representation from outside

<u>For the family</u>

- Wrote a family mission statement
- Ensured that the family values are transmitted to each generation
- Developed career paths for other family members

⌘   ⌘   ⌘

Checklist

✓ Do all you can to foster and maintain the health and well-being of the family.

✓ Use good advice and counsel to make wise decisions in line with a well-crafted business strategy.

✓ When needed, use professional managers to bring the business to the next level.

✓ Use governance structures that will work for your situation: a board, a family council, or family meetings.

✓ Develop employment practices for family members entering the business.

✓ Develop a "code of conduct" for the family.

✓ Write a mission statement.

✓ Use all the tools at your disposal to grow the business, its leaders, and the family.

✓ Compile the family cookbook!

Eight

Communicate, Plan, Act

We have arrived

The overarching Message of this book is: communicate with each other, plan the transition in leadership (and all other aspects of a succession plan), and most importantly, *act.*

The families you have read about faced a particular set of challenges when developing their next generation of business leaders. Either they found a way to meet those challenges in a way that worked for them and their circumstances, or they did not. The Ericksons, for example, were completely unprepared for dealing with the consequences when Carl suddenly died. With the Barbosa family, the fact that the kids were not quite ready to take over the business led them to install a nonfamily CEO. This decision, by far, was the critical turning point in the history of their business and its success. Their recognition that they not only needed time to develop the kids, but also needed to professionalize their leadership was a monumental decision. The time and energy to work through all of the sticky issues associated with such a decision was well worth the time and effort. Many family enterprises never get through this phase successfully, resulting in the sale of a once-successful business and the unraveling of a once-cohesive family.

> Communicate with each other, plan the transition in leadership, and, most importantly, *act.*

Below are the families that we have met, along with a snapshot of their story and the resolution they reached (or did not.)

1. Erickson Family	When Carl dropped dead everything stopped. The family and *Erickson Sealants* limped along but never recovered from the devastating loss.
2. Cleary Family	Mary is diagnosed with Alzheimer's disease. Bill develops a plan to transition *Cleary Floors*. The children take over and run the business.
3. Morelli Family	For new immigrants, the *Bambino Carriage Company* becomes a great success. The family learns how to use advisers and get the education they need to run the company. Rosa and Pina lead the business.
4. Sparks Family	*Sparks Family Enterprises* is unified in their commitment to building the business, doing good, and giving back to the community. They develop a business model and leadership plan with the siblings in the business. Stan uses executive coaching for leadership development.
5. Barbosa Family	The family restaurant blossoms into an empire that spans several businesses. The succession process and development of the next generation of leaders is a transparent process. The nonfamily CEO helps lead the family and its enterprises in a smooth leadership transition.
6. Bluestone Family	A multigenerational family infused with selfishness, arrogance, and small-mindedness, the Bluestones have no operating business. With the death of mother, they showed their true colors. Not an American family success story. There is no development of business or family leaders. A sad mess.

7. Gladney Family   *An American family success story.* A family rooted in hard work, tradition, and strong will, they built a business that spans four generations. Determination and commitment to family are the hallmarks of this family. They developed their family and business leaders who brought the business and the family into the modern era.

Plan, Communicate, and Act

- **The big picture**

  The big picture is what you have in mind for the future of the business and the continued well-being of the family. This vision is tied to the strategic plan of the business and is rooted in the culture and values of the family. The Erickson family, perhaps had a big picture view for the future, but it died with Carl. The vision must be worked on, communicated, and become part of the fabric of the family and its business. The Sparks family developed and communicated a unified vision. Everyone knew what that was and what he or she was contributing to achieve that goal.

- **Take one step**

  The first step is the hardest. Where to start? Get all interested parties—everyone with a stake of some sort in the business—and call a meeting to discuss the business and its future. There is only one place to start, and that's wherever you are right now.

- **Talk to each other**

  Talk to each other more than you think is necessary. The more the message that "we need to communicate with each other" gets out there, the less resistance there will be to it. There is no right way to do it, except to start somewhere. Lunch on Wednesday is one place to start or breakfast meetings once a month.

- **Talk to other families**

  Other families can be a great source of knowledge, inspiration and support when considering a transition in the business. Talking with families who "have been there" gives you a sounding board and someone who has the experience and is a bit further down the road. Whether accomplished in the formal context of a family business center or informally by developing and reaching out to a network of family businesses, these connections can be of great help in getting you going and keeping you focused on your own transition and the development of your leaders.

- **Meet and greet consultants and advisers**

  Family business consultants and advisers are there to be of help. Good ones know what they are good at. They can be a cost-effective way of the keeping you on track, helping you stick with your plan (once it is developed) and guiding you to see all the options you have.

- **Use your trusted advisers**

  All of your trusted advisers should be behind you in your plan. Some will resist and will want to stick with the way "things have always been." The alignment of the advisers with each other will help you enormously in developing your plan and seeing it through. Remember, this is not a sprint to the finish. It is a long, and sometimes troubling, frustrating process. Family members need to be aligned with the business and family goals.

- **Listen to the people who know something**

  Everyone has opinions. This is fine. You need to be talking with people who know what they are talking about, have been there before, and believe in what you are trying to accomplish. The naysayers will not help you. The idea is to keep moving forward

● **Construct a timetable**

Where do you want to be in two years, in five years? As we have seen with the Gladney family and many of the families in this book, there always needs to be timetable, with goals tied to it. It is not enough to say "Jane will take over the business when she is ready." Her development needs to be clearly defined and tied to goals and expectations of what Jane should be doing to prepare and develop herself to become the next CEO of the company. The development plans of Rosa and Pina Morelli, for example, is a good place to start for formulating ideas about what a development plan looks like.

⌘ ⌘ ⌘

Use the checklist from the previous chapter

✓ Do all you can to foster and maintain the health and well-being of the family.

✓ Use good advice and counsel to make wise decisions in line with a well-crafted business strategy.

✓ When needed, use professional managers to bring the business to the next level.

✓ Use governance structures that will work for you situation: a board, a family council, or family meetings.

✓ Develop employment practices for family members entering the business.

✓ Develop a "code of conduct" for the family.

✓ Write a mission statement.

✓ Use all the tools at your disposal to grow the business, its leaders, and the family.

✓ Have some fun!

A final observation

Stan Sparks, of *Sparks Family Enterprises*, engaged in and dug deep in to the executive coaching relationship as a springboard to developing his skills as leader of his management team. Reaching an "aha" moment in his work with this coach, he offered a telling observation about his development efforts. He remarked, "You know, this $@%# works!"

Yes, it does.

⌘   ⌘   ⌘

Some family trees have beautiful leaves, and some have just a bunch of nuts. Remember, it is the nuts that make the tree worth shaking.

~ Another Yet-To-Be-Named Wise Person

Nine

Resources

Recommended Books

Aronoff, Craig, Stephen McClure, and John L. Ward *Family Business Succession: The Final Test of Greatness,* second ed. (Family Business Consulting Group, 2003).

Aronoff, Craig and John L. Ward *Family Meetings: How to Build a Stronger Family and a Stronger Business* (Family Enterprise Publishers, 2002).

Astrachan, Joseph H. and Kristi S. McMillan *Conflict and Communication in the Family Business* (Family Enterprise Publishers, 2003).

Carlock, R., and John Ward *Strategic Planning for the Family Business: Parallel Planning to Unify the Family Business* (Palgrave, 2001).

George, Bill, Peter Sims, and David Gergen True North: Discover Your Authentic Leadership (Jossey-Bass, 2007).

Gersick, Kelin, John Davis, Marion McCollom Hampton, and Ivan Lansberg *Generation to Generation: Life Cycles of the Family Business* (Boston, MA: Harvard Business School Press, 1997).

Hartley, Bonnie Brown and Gwendolyn Griffith *Family Wealth Transition Planning: Advising Families with Small Businesses* (Bloomberg, 2009).

Hughes, James *Family Wealth—Keeping It in the Family: How Family Members and Their Advisers Preserve Human, Intellectual, and Financial Assets for Generations* (Bloomberg, 2004).

Jaffe, Dennis *Working with Ones You Love* (Conari Press, 1990).

_____ *Stewardship in Your Family Enterprise* (Pioneer Imprints, 2010).

Kets de Vries, M.F.R., and Randel Carlock *Family Business on the Couch* (Wiley, 2007).

Krasnow, Henry *Your Lawyer: An Owner's Manual* (Agate, 2006).

Mason, Jean *Intimate Tyranny: Untangling Father's Legacy* (Centora Press, 2008).

Morris, Richard and Jayne Pearl *Kids, Wealth, and Consequences: Ensuring a Responsible Financial Future for the Next Generation* (Bloomberg Press, 2010).

⌘   ⌘   ⌘

References

Hollander, Barbara and Wendy Bukowitz "Women, Family Culture, and Family Business," *Family Business Review* 3, 2 (1990): 139-151.

Hoy, Frank and Sharma, Pramodita. "Entrepreneurial Governance in the Family Firm," in Barbara Spector, ed., *The Family Business Shareholder's Handbook*. (Philadelphia, PA: Family Business Publishing Co., 2008).

LaChapelle, Kacie, and Louis B. Barnes "The Trust Catalyst in Family-Owned Businesses," *Family Business Review*, 11, 1 (1998): 1-17.

Tagiuri, Renato and Davis, John (1982). "Bivalent attributes of the family firm." Working Paper, Harvard Business School, Cambridge, MA. Reprinted 1996, Family Business Review IX (2) 199-208.

⌘ ⌘ ⌘

Tips for Family Meetings

Step 1: Why?

- Do you need a meeting? Why? Is it in response to some crisis/emergency or what?
- What is the purpose and goal?
- What are the boundaries: just talk about family or only about business? Consider just having dinner together if you just want to get together.

Step 2: Who?

- Who gets invited? Who is calling the meeting?
- If it is a *family* meeting, who is in the family? How do you define the family?

Step 3: What?

- Plan the meeting: where, when, and how. Who will do all this?
- It must be a group effort
- Don't assume anything.
- Should there be a facilitator: if so, should it be a family member or an outsider?

Step 4: The Meeting

- Create an agenda: keep it simple.
- Agree on who will facilitate the discussion (take the lead).
- Set the timetable with beginning and ending time, and stick to it.
- Always have ground rules for discussion; for example, only one person speaks at a time, make **"I"** statements (as in "I think that we should have a committee to create an employment plan for the next generation") not *you*

statements (as in "You can't mean that? You have always been...").

- Brainstorm ideas; encourage differing ideas.
- Narrow down solutions.
- Consider the pros and cons for the family and the business.
- Arrive at a solution and follow through.

⌘ ⌘ ⌘

Family Business Centers in the United States and Canada

Family Business Centers

United States

Auburn University Lowder Center for Family Business and Entrepreneurship Auburn,   AL

University of Arkansas - Fort Smith   Fort Smith   AR

University of Central Arkansas   Small Business Advancement National Center Conway   AR

Thunderbird School of Global Management Global Family Enterprise Program   Glendale   AZ

California State University Bakersfield Family Business Institute Bakersfield CA

California State University Fresno Institute for Family Business   Fresno   CA

California State University Fullerton Fullerton   CA

California State University Northridge Family Business Education and Research Center   Northridge   CA

San Diego State University   EMC Business Forum   San Diego   CA

San Francisco State University Family Enterprise Center   San Diego   CA

Stanford Graduate School of Business Stanford   CA

University of San Diego Family Business Forum   San Diego   CA

University of San Francisco   San Francisco   CA

University of the Pacific Institute for Family Business Stockton   CA

University of Connecticut   Storrs   CT

University of New Haven   West Haven   CT

George Washington University Center for Entrepreneurial Excellence (CFEE) Washington DC

National Association of Corporate Directors (NACD) Washington DC

Florida Gulf Coast University Small Business Development Center Fort Meyers FL

Florida International University Eugenio Pino & Family Global Entrepreneurship Center Miami FL

Florida State University The Jim Moran Institute for Global Entrepreneurship Tallahassee FL

Nova Southeastern University Ft. Lauderdale FL

Stetson University Deland FL

The University of Tampa Florida Entrepreneurship Center Tampa FL

U.S. Association for Small Business and Entrepreneurship (USASBE) Boca Raton FL

Georgia State University Atlanta GA

Kennesaw State University Cox Family Enterprise Center Kennesaw GA

University of Hawaii Honolulu HI

Iowa State University Small Business Development Center Ames IA

AFHE (Attorneys for Family-Held Enterprises) Schaumberg IL

DePaul University Entrepreneurship Program Chicago IL

Loyola University Chicago Chicago IL

Northwestern University Kellogg School of Management Center for Family Enterprises Evanston IL

University of Illinois at Chicago Family Business Council Chicago IL

Goshen College Goshen IN

University of Notre Dame Gigot Center for Entrepreneurial Studies Notre Dame   IN

Wichita State University   Wichita   KS

Northern Kentucky University – Small Business Development Center Highland Heights   KY

University of Kentucky Kentucky   Small Business Development Center   Lexington   KY

University of Louisville   Family Business Center/College of Business Louisville   KY

Louisiana State University Stephenson Entrepreneurship Institute Baton Rouge   LA

Tulane University Tulane University Family Business Center New Orleans   LA

University of Louisiana at Monroe Family Business Institute Monroe   LA

Babson College Arthur M. Blank Center for Entrepreneurship Babson Park   MA

Boston University Institute for Technology Entrepreneurship and Commercialization Boston   MA

Harvard University Business School - Families in Business: From Generation to Generation Program Boston   MA

Harvard University Business School   Owner/President Management Program (OPM)   Boston   MA

Northeastern University Center for Family Business Boston   MA

Suffolk University Sawyer School of Management Boston   MA

University of Massachusetts, Amherst   Family Business Center Hadley   MA

Worcester Polytechnic Institute Worcester   MA

Loyola University Maryland   Center for Closely Held Firms Baltimore   MD

Institute for Family-Owned Business Portland   ME

Family Business Council (SE Michigan) West Bloomfield   MI

Grand Valley State University Family Owned Business Institute
     Grand Rapids   MI

University of Michigan – Flint Michigan Family Business Center
     Flint   MI

Michigan   Small   Business   &   Technology   Development
     Center   Grand Rapids   MI

Saginaw Valley State University   Center for Family Business
     University Center   MI

Walsh College Troy   MI

Family Enterprise USA Minneapolis   MN

University of St. Thomas   Family Business Center
     Minneapolis   MN

St. Louis University Smurfit-Stone Center for Entrepreneurship St.
     Louis   MO

Mississippi State University   Mississippi State   MS

Montana State University   Bozeman   MT

University of North Carolina at Asheville The Family Business
     Forum Asheville   NC

University of North Carolina Family Enterprise Institute, Center
     for Entrepreneurial Studies Kenan-Flagler Business School
     Chapel Hill,   NC

University of North Carolina at Greensboro   Department of
     Business Administration Greensboro   NC

Wake Forest University Family Business Center   Winston-
     Salem   NC

Creighton   University   Center   for   Family   Business
     Omaha   NE

University of Nebraska Nebraska Center for Entrepreneurship
     Lincoln   NE

University of New Hampshire   Center for Family Business
     Durham   NH

Fairleigh Dickinson University   Family Business Forum
Madison   NJ

Rutgers University School of Business Camden   NJ

William Paterson University   Center for Closely Held Businesses
Wayne   NJ

Baruch College Lawrence N. Field Center for Entrepreneurship
New York   NY

Canisius College Women's Business Center Buffalo   NY

New York University   New York   NY

Pace University Small Business Development Center   New
York   NY

The State University of New York at Buffalo   Center for
Entrepreneurial Leadership   Buffalo   NY

Case Western Reserve University Cleveland   OH

Conway Center for Family Business Columbus   OH

University of Cincinnati Goering Center for Family and Private
Business Cincinnati OH

The University of Toledo Toledo   OH

University of Oklahoma Entrepreneurship Center Norman   OK

University of Tulsa Family-Owned Business Institute Tulsa   OK

Delaware Valley Family Business Center Telford   PA

Elizabethtown College   S. Dale High Center for Family
Business   Elizabethtown   PA

Kings College   Family Business Forum, William G. McGowan
School of Business   Wilkes-Barre   PA

Seton Hill University   Women's Business Center
Greensburg   PA

Temple University Small Business Development Center
Philadelphia   PA

The American College Bryn Mawr   PA

University of Pennsylvania   Wharton Global Family Alliance
Philadelphia PA

University of Pittsburgh Institute for Entrepreneurial Excellence Pittsburgh PA

Bryant University Smithfield   RI

University of South Dakota Sioux Falls   SD

Belmont University   Center for Entrepreneurship Nashville   TN

Tennessee Family Business Center Nashville   TN

Baylor University   The Institute for Family Business Waco   TX

Texas A&M University Center for New Ventures and Entrepreneurship College Station   TX

Texas Tech University Center for Entrepreneurship and Family Business Lubbock TX

Brigham Young University   Center for Entrepreneurship Provo   UT

Virginia Commonwealth University Virginia Family & Private Business Forum Richmond VA

University of Vermont   Vermont Family Business Initiative Burlington   VT

Pacific Lutheran University   Tacoma   WA

University of Wisconsin - Green Bay   Small Business Development Center   Green Bay   WI

University of Wisconsin – Madison Madison   WI

University of Wisconsin – Oshkosh   Wisconsin Family Business Forum Oshkosh WI

Family Business Centers

Canada

Lethbridge College Family Life Studies Program Lethbridge   AB

University of Alberta   Alberta Business Family Institute (ABFI) Edmonton   AB

University of Alberta School of Business Edmonton   AB

University of Calgary Calgary   AB

University of British Columbia Business Families Centre Vancouver   BC

University of Manitoba   Department of Family Social Sciences Winnipeg   MB

Dalhousie University   School of Business Administration Halifax   NS

Brock University St. Catherines   ON

Canadian Association of Family Enterprise (CAFÉ) Oakville   ON

Ryerson University Loretta Rogers Chair of Entrepreneurship Research Toronto   ON

University of Waterloo   Centre For Family Business (CFFB) Waterloo   ON

Wilfrid Laurier University The Schlegel Centre for Entrepreneurship Waterloo ON

York University Toronto   ON

Concordia University   The Centre for Small Business and Entrepreneurial Studies (CSBES) Montreal   QC

Concordia University   Montreal   QC

HEC Montréal Montreal   QC

McGill University The Dobson Center for Entrepreneurial Studies Montreal   QC

⌘ ⌘ ⌘

About the author

Gerard J. Donnellan, PhD

Gerry Donnellan is president and founder of *Big Leap (www.big-leap.com)*, a consulting company that utilizes innovative approaches in working with family and closely-held businesses. Trained as a clinical psychologist and psychoanalyst, he has over thirty-five years of professional experience. As an organizational consulting psychologist and family business consultant, he works with families and their businesses as they navigate their way through the ups and downs of owning and running their businesses, all while hoping they all will still want to be together for Thanksgiving dinner.

He is adjunct professor at the International Business School of Brandeis University and has held university faculty appointments at Harvard Medical School and the City University of New York. He was founding director of the Institute for Organizational Consulting Psychology at the Massachusetts School of Professional Psychology (MSPP), Boston.

He was awarded the *Certificate in Family Business Advising* by the Family Firm Institute (FFI). He is on the faculty of the certificate program and is a frequent presenter at FFI conferences.

Gerry lives in Lexington, Massachusetts.

Made in the USA
Charleston, SC
22 June 2011